HOLD MY HAND,

Lord!

4-30-19

Tina & Joran,

I hope my story will
encourage you to write
your story.

May our Lord continue
to bless you & yours!

I love you so much &
all your family!

xoo

Mom

Hold My Hand,
Lord!

My Journey Through Cancers

GWEN HENSLEY

WESTBOW
PRESS®
A DIVISION OF THOMAS NELSON
& ZONDERVAN

WestBow Press books may be ordered through booksellers or by contacting:

WestBow Press
A Division of Thomas Nelson & Zondervan
1663 Liberty Drive
Bloomington, IN 47403
www.westbowpress.com
1 (866) 928-1240

KJV: Unless otherwise cited, scriptures taken from the King James Version of the Bible.

NKJV: Scripture taken from the New King James Version®. Copyright © 1982 by Thomas Nelson. Used by permission. All rights reserved.

ISBN: 978-1-9736-5838-2 (sc)
ISBN: 978-1-9736-5839-9 (hc)
ISBN: 978-1-9736-5837-5 (e)

Library of Congress Control Number: 2019903682

Print information available on the last page.

WestBow Press rev. date: 4/11/2019

My story is dedicated to my five wonderful adult children and their families:

Gayla
Gary
Gina
Glynne'
Raymond

and to my deceased husband, Earle, now living in Heaven

"...Your right hand has held me up..."
Psalm 18:35 (NKJV)

No matter what happens to you, please do **not** give up.

Reach for our Lord's hand. Let Him lead you through life's storms into His sunshine.

May the Holy Spirit bless each of you as you go through daily life. May He encourage you to daily read our Father's Word, the Holy Bible, and talk to Him in prayer through Jesus Christ, His only Son and our Savior.

Thank you for the privilege of sharing my story with you.

Contents

CHAPTER 1

HERE WE GO AGAIN

H ere we go again. It's Tuesday, May 15, 2007. My oncologist, Dr. Bassam Mattar, has just told me that the "area" is growing again and I need to go back into chemotherapy treatments. What a shock. I feel so good. My energy is back – somewhat, anyway. My hair is growing back and my fingernails are growing back. I feel like living again and making plans for the future. Okay, so now what? But the good news is I may be a candidate for the new CyberKnife radiation treatment. I have to do some research on this. More good news is this growth has been caught in its very early stages. It did not show up on the Computed Tomography (CT) scan or in the Carcino Embryonic Antigen (CEA), a cancer marker in the blood. It did show up on the Positron Emission Tomography (PET) scan. This means we have caught it early. It's small. Dr. Mattar is prepared to fight it again with me. Now, I wonder, is the Good Lord still trying to tell me something I am just not getting yet? Or, is there some other good result He wants to happen from this third recurrence of colorectal cancer in me? Or, is this the path I am to take as He calls me home to Heaven? I do not know. Mine is not to know or try to figure out. My job is to accept the fact that God has allowed this to happen to me again. I am to trust in Him. I am to hold on to His Hand as He lifts and carries me through this wild ride called "life".

Life is a journey here on earth, our temporary home. Our eternal home is Heaven. On our journey, there are many obstacles in our path. Some are good and wonderful. Some are bad and terrible. But as we travel, we learn that our Savior Jesus Christ has gone before us, showing us the way. He will travel with us now if we let Him. He will remove the obstacles or give us the ability to move beyond them. Either way, we can continue on our road to Heaven. I have an obstacle called cancer that our good Lord is helping me combat. Let me share with you how He has held my hand in the past, and is holding my hand right now, and will continue to hold my hand in the future.

Hold my hand, Lord!

Chapter 2

My First Cancer

I n May of 1975, I was preparing for our second child, Gary, to be confirmed at our church. Our oldest daughter, Gayla, was confirmed the previous year. I had no idea of what I was facing when our family doctor, Dr. Gerhart Tonn, called me into his office. After getting the results of my recent pap smear, he gave me the news that I had **cervical cancer, a squamous cell carcinoma, Stage One, my first cancer.**

Hold my hand, Lord. I need You to be with me.

Needless to say, my precious soul-mate husband, Earle, was as shocked as me. But, as I told the doctor, I had things to do. First, I wanted to be at Gary's confirmation later that month. Dr. Tonn allowed me to do so. Then the radiation treatments began. I had one month of daily cobalt radiation treatments, three X-ray radiation treatments, and two radium implants. The radium implants took forty-eight hours each, two weeks apart. These treatments completely drained my energy.

I remembered, though, that I had been a single mother with four children to raise all by myself: Gayla, Gary, Gina, and Glynne'. I had prayed and asked God to not let anything happen to me until the children were adults. I never wanted my children to be separated. I wanted them to be raised together as a family. I loved them so much. I was totally afraid that if something happened to me, no one would take all four children to rear. They would be split up. So, I prayed for God to keep me alive to keep them together until they could live on their own.

I knew that God had answered my prayer and provided for us when Earle came into our lives. Earle and I fell in love. We got married. When we had our baby, Raymond, we felt our sweet little family was complete. Earle called my parents to let them know our family was complete. My mother answered the phone. He told her, "Well, Mom, they're all mine now!" And they truly were his. He was the best earthly father to all of them. He loved them. He cared for them. He raised them in the church to know the Lord. He taught them about life. He made and built toys for them. He patiently helped each of them through the various stages of growing up, including all the pains and joys. We were so full of love for each other and for all five children. Of course, my brother, Clarence "Chip," has still not forgiven me for not waiting until he returned from Viet Nam to be at our wedding.

Please forgive me, Lord. Bless my brother for his love for me and then for Earle. And thank You, Lord, for placing Earle in our lives.

I knew my children would be fine without me now, as long as they had Earle. So, I accepted what God had allowed to happen to me. I thought He was through with me here on earth. I thought my journey was complete and my Lord would take me home to Heaven.

Thank You, Lord, for providing for my children and me. Please hold Earle's hand, too, Lord, and our children's hands. They may have to go through the rest of their lives without me.

Then came the third X-ray radiation treatment. I was in this big room hooked up to this huge machine, with bright lights everywhere. I was all by myself. The doctor and nurses were watching me through a tiny little lead window. This window protected them from the radiation rays. I was praying, which is what I most always did when I had no distractions. Suddenly, it became pitch black in the room. There was no noise except the humming of the X-ray machine. I felt a shudder go through my body. Then it was absolutely quiet. Even the humming of the machine had stopped. There was a peace gently surrounding me.

Immediately, a man's voice, authoritative and matter-of-fact, said to me, **"Gwen, you're going to be okay."**

I was stunned! Then, the bright lights again filled the room. The hum of the machine returned until the treatment was complete.

As they wheeled me out of the room, my radiologist asked me how I was doing, as he always did. I told him that I was going to be okay. God had told me so. He looked straight into my eyes and told me he believed me. And the bleeding stopped. But I still had to continue with and complete the two radium implant treatments. This happened about a month after the other two types of treatments. I had to be in the hospital – lay flat on my back and not move – for forty-eight hours each while the radium pellets did their work inside me. The radium treatments were about two weeks apart.

Keep holding my hand, Lord. This is all new to me.

I had some difficulty – mostly emotional – with the first radium implant. So, I wasn't looking forward to the second implant. I was quite upset. My wonderful hubby took me in his arms. He told me, "Honey, I know this is rough. But just look to the end. Look to the good results that will happen as the radiation does its job and gets rid of the cancer. I will be right here with you and so will God." And, he was with me through the completion of both treatments.

Hold Earle's hand and my hand too, Lord.

From this support I was able to make it through the remainder of the treatments. I was given a clean bill of health. **I was cured from my first cancer.**

Thank You, Lord, for this blessing also. What an awesome God you are!

However, Dr. Tonn told me that since I only had radiation and no surgery, I would probably need to have a hysterectomy in twenty years – I would be fifty-five years old – or by the time I was sixty years old. I could live with that very easily. Those years were way down the line in the future. I could not see or think or care about something that far ahead. I was still alive. I had a family to care for now.

Keep holding my hand, Lord.

I also thank God for my parents, Clarence "Hank" and Marie, while I was in the hospital. Even though they lived out of town, they were able to come to our home and help take care of the children. All five were such good children. I struggled through these treatments, physically and emotionally. The treatments had left me with little or no energy to take care of our children.

Thank You, Lord, for knowing what I needed better than I knew myself.

CHAPTER 3

PAIN AND SIDE EFFECTS OF CANCER

We were so busy taking care of me that only my mother noticed something was wrong with Gina's back. The doctor's examination revealed she had scoliosis, a curvature of the spine. Treatment for her began immediately. She was fitted for a back brace and was given a list of exercises to do twice a day. She was such an excellent patient. She did everything the doctor told her to do. The other kids would get down on the floor with her and do her exercises with her. I know that helped her so much.

Thank You, Lord, for my mom and the doctor and for the other kids helping Gina. Thank You for holding Gina's hands as she struggled through her teen-age years with this problem.

During this time, it was all I could do just to drive myself to the hospital and undergo the cobalt and X-ray treatments. Then I would drive home and just sit in the rocking chair, too exhausted even to cook. Earle did everything. He was great, such a blessing to all of us.

Thank You, Lord, for my wonderful Honey Earle, my parents, and my children.

Life was wonderful, busy, frustrating and fun. Everything that life is when you have a large family. We moved to a small town. We were blessed with our first grandchild, Joshua, in 1978.

Thank You, Lord, for this first of many grandchildren. Bless him and all of us.

But, in late 1982 – with only one offspring left at home – I started having pain in my back that would not go away. I had never had pain like this. Gary was playing football at a local university – set two school records as wide receiver, by the way. We would drive to his games. Sometimes on the way to games I would be hurting so much, I would cry. This really upset Raymond. Dr. Tonn tried everything to relieve my pain and so did I. Finally, one medicine he prescribed for me made me so sick (vomiting, etc.) that I could not take it anymore. I had to ask Raymond to call the ambulance for me. Earle was in class. He and I were taking Emergency Medical Technician (EMT) courses at a local community college. I had begged Earle to go ahead to the class that night and take notes for me too. I had told him not to worry, that I would be all right. So he did go, reluctantly. But I wasn't okay. I hurt so badly, I forgot to pray!

Raymond called his dad and told him what happened. Earle was very shocked and very upset. He and Raymond came immediately to the hospital Emergency Room (ER). It took three shots of a powerful pain killer – Demerol, I think – to even begin to ease my pain. The doctors could not figure out what was wrong. The EMTs thought I had kidney stones. This made good sense since the pain was in my back. We found out later that the pain was not from kidney stones. It was a result of damage by scar tissues from my previous radiation treatments. When the pain began subsiding, I went to sleep. I was in the hospital eight days, sleeping most of the time. The doctors ran all kinds of tests on me. I cannot tell you which ones, because I would only wake up when they told me they were doing something to me. Then I would go right back to sleep. They thought it was the cancer coming back on me, but it wasn't. No one could tell me what went wrong or what caused the pain.

Hold my hand, Lord.

After I got out of the hospital, Dr. Tonn had me come to his office. He performed a dilatation of the cervix (D&C), right in his office, with no anesthetic. He drained approximately one-half pint of fluids from what was left of my uterus. He explained to me that the scar tissue from the radiations had closed off the cervix. Then, because the uterus had not been completely destroyed by the radiations, it began filling up a little bit every month. The fluids accumulating inside had made the uterus tilt back on my sacroiliac ligament. This caused muscle spasms which were extremely painful, very similar to constant labor. No pain medicines would help. After Dr. Tonn completed the draining procedure, the pain was gone in just a few minutes. I only had cramps for a couple of hours. I was amazed that good ole Dr. Tonn figured this out when the cancer doctors could not. Dr. Tonn also told me to never let the pain get that bad again. He told me to come back and get it taken care of immediately. I promised I would. No problem there.

Life again returned to "normal" and was wonderful. We began having more grandchildren, Tarah and James.

Praise be to You, Lord. Thank You for the blessings of these beautiful babies and for holding our hands, Lord.

CHAPTER 4

MY SECOND CANCER

On November 3, 1990, my precious mother died of lung cancer after being diagnosed in August. This was a terrible blow to my father, brother, me, and all of our families.

Hold our hands, Lord. Part of our family is now missing. We've never experienced this before.

We all felt that Mom knew about this much longer than she ever would admit. But she wanted to keep it to herself. We were comforted by the fact that Mom knew Jesus. We trusted that she was in Heaven with Him and not suffering anymore. Still, the separation of her earthly life left us confused. We wanted to see her, talk to her, and hug her. But that is not possible. Her death was a final separation from earth and from us. We had to accept the fact that we could not talk to her again until we got to Heaven. That's such a permanent realization. Earthly life had to go on without her. This event – her illness and death – brought my brother and me close together again. Our busy lives had kept us apart for a while.

Thank You, Lord, for the blessing of my brother and my mother – with such a strong faith. Thank You for a mother who was a very strong woman in everything she set out to accomplish. She taught me that I could do and be anything I wanted, if I really worked hard and looked to You for guidance.

In 1992, I started getting that same type of pain in my back again. I knew it was time to return to the doctor. Since Dr. Tonn had retired, I began seeing Dr. Kimberly Hartwell, another great doctor. And I love her too. She said it was time to see the oncology surgeon again.

Hold my hand, Lord.

So, back to the gynecological oncologist I went. He had been an intern in 1975 during my first bout with cancer. He had taken good care of me at that time. He also was my gynecological oncologist in 1982. Tests and examinations disclosed the fact that I needed to have a hysterectomy, and I needed to have it now. The surgery should be completed before more scar tissue from the three different radiations (cobalt, radium and X-ray) did any more damage. I was in good health. I was just finally getting my Associates Degree in Business Administration from a local community college. It only took me thirty-four years to get a two-year college degree – ha. All five children were graduated from high school, Gayla, Gary, Gina, Glynne', and Raymond.

They were getting settled in life. We were grandparents and enjoying it very much: Joshua, Tarah, James, Jared, and Rachael.

Earle and I prayed about this suggested hysterectomy. We decided to go ahead with the surgery. Before I was even fully awake from the anesthetic, the doctor surgeon came into my room. I was still a little groggy when he told us that the pathology report showed there was a malignant tumor inside what was left of the uterus they had removed. The tumor was completely contained within the uterus. It had not penetrated through the uterus wall. It was entirely encapsulated inside the uterus.

Thank You, Lord, for holding our hands through this unexpected news.

This **uterine cancer, an adenocarcinoma, a cancer of the gland, was my second cancer.** I would require no further treatment. **I was considered cured from this cancer also.**

Thank You, Lord, for holding my hand and the hands of the doctors.

Life again returned back to normal, whatever normal is. More grandchildren came along: Mariah, Tanner, and Trae. We also were blessed with great-grandsons: Gage and Braden. My brother, Chip, and his wife, Fran, also had grandchildren: Bailey, Sydney, Kelsey, and Tucker.

Thank You, Lord, for the blessings of more beautiful babies to love.

CHAPTER 5

FAMILY LIFE AND ADVENTURES

However, a terrible event happened in June 1998. Our precious daughter, Gayla, had an aneurysm behind her left eye on the optic nerve. This required major brain surgery, followed by weeks of recuperation. This devastated Earle and me and our entire family. Earle was literally sick with worry. As her father, this was something he could not fix. It was so hard for all of our family, waiting for the surgery, knowing that at any time something very bad could happen to her. We finally gave our daughter's life over to the Lord. The Lord did take care of her. Gayla has written her story, so I'll let her tell you. It's a good one. We were just so grateful to God that she lived through this and is still doing well. I do remember one thing Gayla said while she was in the Intensive Care Unit (ICU). She doesn't remember saying this to me, "I'm going to be okay, Mom. It's not right that a mother should lose her child." The Lord healed her completely.

Thank You, Lord, for sparing our daughter and for holding her hand and all our hands through this terrible and frightening ordeal. Continue to bless her life also.

In November 1998, Earle had back surgery. He decided to retire in December of 1998, as Under Sheriff of our county. So, I followed suit and retired also. However, I waited until the next year in 1999. We spent some wonderful time together for a couple of years. We were enjoying each other's company, traveling, visiting friends and family, etc. We just did whatever we wanted to do, whenever we wanted. In 1999, we also went to the races at Texas Motor Speedway which Earle loved. Another great-grandson, Garrett, was born. Also, we shopped. Oh, how Earle loved to shop and people-watch.

Now that I look back on those days, I can see where the good Lord was blessing us with precious memories. He brought people from the past back into our lives, especially Earle's. One man he had served with in the U.S. Marine Corps during the 1950's came to Kansas and found Earle. They spent time together getting reacquainted and reminiscing. Earle so enjoyed that. Also, people he had arrested years ago when he was a law enforcement officer would greet him. They told tell him they appreciated what he did for them, and that Earle had helped them to turn their life around. They would thank him. Earle was amazed, but grateful, for their comments. He was a humble and good man. I was told later that people looked up to us and our marriage and our family. I, too, was surprised. We never thought about any of this. We just tried to live our lives as we thought God would want us to live. We wanted to get through all the trials, tribulations, joys, and happiness with God's help. We wanted to stay together, to build each other up, and to enjoy this wonderful ride through life.

Hold our hands, Lord.

In March of 2000, Earle and I went to visit our daughter, Gayla, and her family, including two of her grandsons, Gage and Garrett. Somehow as I was carrying baby Garrett down the stairs to the basement where we were gathering, I missed the last step. I heard two pops and my legs collapsed. I fell forward and just rolled Garrett out on the floor. He looked up at me as if to say "Hey, that was fun; let's do it again." However, Earle did not say that. He was totally upset and grabbed the baby, who really was just fine. I had protected the baby by landing on my knees first, then my elbows, and then just rolling Garrett out on the carpeted floor. I knew instantly it was not going to hurt the baby, but it was going to hurt me. Sure enough, after we got to the ER, tests showed I had sprained both ankles and broken the left one. What a surprise. The doctor asked if I was an athlete – ha. He said I had a hairline fracture like athletes get. So, I had to wear an ankle/leg brace for several weeks. I even wore the brace on our trip to Dallas to the Texas Motor Speedway races. But first, I had to take lessons on how to walk in a foot brace and how to use crutches – Crutches 101. But, I healed quickly and completely.

Thank You, Lord. I remember You are the Great Physician.

Then, in about May of 2000, I began having problems again. I refused to think about it and just went on with life. There was so much to do with family and extended family. My dad was in a nursing home near my brother's home. I was involved in church work, volunteer work, etc. We traveled in August out of state to visit our grandson, Joshua, his wife, and two boys, Gage and Garrett. What fun we had. We also traveled to another state with cousins, LaVada – and her husband Carl – and Dolores – and her husband Charles. We had such a great time with them. It was on this trip that I sneaked under the roped-off area in a car museum to get pictures of a 1948 Buick Super for Earle. He could not believe I would do that for him. He had bought a 1948 Buick Super from my dad and wanted to restore it back to original just like the one in the museum. He needed the pictures to help him see what it should look like. So, I got them for him. Unfortunately, he never got to do this. But at least he knew how much I dearly loved him.

Thank You for Earle, our grandchildren, all our cousins, and wonderful memories, Lord.

In August 2000, the nursing home in our small town contacted me about having a monthly Bible study/songfest for the residents. Of course, I called my Pastor Brack and talked to him about it. He told me to "go for it." So, I did. With the help of many friends, we started in August 2000 and still continue today. I've only missed two days. One day was on the day of my second colon surgery. The other day I missed was because I was just too sick from the chemotherapy treatments to even stand up. This Bible study/songfest has been a blessing for me much more than for the residents. They are so appreciative. And I have been blessed with the most wonderful friends to help me each month: Velda, Gloria (who plays the piano), Mary, and Verba. They are still very dedicated. And there are others who help occasionally.

Thank You, Lord, for these faithful friends and their dedication to Your Word, the Holy Bible.

Then, we took the trip of a lifetime – at least for me it was. I think it also was for Earle. In September 2000, we traveled back east to visit our daughter, Gina, and her family. Gina's husband, Goran, was a professional soccer player in Philadelphia. Goran drove all of us, Earle, Gina, Tarah, Tanner, Trae, and me, to Atlantic City. We played by the ocean and smelled the salty air. We climbed over rocks and picked up shells. We walked the boardwalk. Goran also drove us to Philadelphia. We toured the U.S. Mint – a great and fascinating place. We also toured all the historical buildings. We visited the Liberty Bell. Then Goran drove us to the Statue of Liberty. We went inside and walked up as far as they would let us. Earle made the remark that he never thought he would get to see the Statue of Liberty, let alone actually be there and touch her. We took the ferry to Ellis Island. This also made a big impression on Earle. He was so into history and military stuff – Earle was a former U.S. Marine. We saw military ships and toured museums, etc.

Before we left the docks by the Statue of Liberty, Earle asked me to take a picture of him standing on the dock. He wanted to have the World Trade Center/Twin Towers in the background.

Those buildings were way across the bay. So, I did what he wanted. That picture was taken September 14, 2000. It is a great picture. Our family and many friends have copies of this special picture. Little did we know that three months and two days later, Earle would be gone from us. And, less than one year later, the Twin Towers would be gone as well. We all sadly remember our nation's infamous nine-eleven. Looking back, we realize it is a very good thing that we do not know what the future has in store for us. But we have precious memories.

Hold my hand, Lord. I don't know what the future holds, but I do know Who holds the future.

After leaving the Statue of Liberty, Goran drove us under the bay waters through the tunnels to the Twin Towers. We toured those towers also. Of course, Earle, being Earle – if you only knew how claustrophobic and paranoid Earle was – just about panicked as we were going up in the elevator. Some guy made a smart-aleck remark about the elevators not working properly lately. They were getting stuck between floors. Most of us laughed because we knew that guy was just kidding. But, Earle did not laugh. However, it is a fact that the elevator only goes up one hundred seven stories, due to the space required for the mechanics. We had to get out of the elevator and walk up the stairs for the last three stories. Then, we walked out into the breath-taking night air with clouds literally enveloping us. It was eerily and absolutely beautiful. We could not even see the other tower. Only the red light on the top of the other tower was barely visible sometimes through the clouds that surrounded us. It was surreal and awesome. And again, Earle made the remark about getting to see and touch something he always wanted to, but never thought he would actually get to. We had many other wonderful memories from these trips and visits.

Thank You, Lord. You are so good to us. You give us laughter, enjoyment, amazement, and love.

Chapter 6

My Third Cancer

As we were traveling home, it became painfully clear to me that I needed to go back to the doctor. So I did. The news was not good. I needed surgery on my colon as something was blocking it. Dr. Hartwell sent me to a great surgeon, Dr. Diane Hunt. I came to love her also. My family and I were all in her conference room asking questions and getting information. She explained to us that I would need to have part of my colon removed and replaced with a colostomy. It would be a temporary colostomy if they could find enough good tissue to reconnect the sections in a few months after I healed. But, if they could not, the colostomy would have to be permanent. Again, we prayed.

Hold my hand, Lord. I still desperately need Your help.

In the meantime, our daughter, Gayla, took me to meet a friend of hers who had a similar situation as mine. This was a big help. However, I was overwhelmed with all this new and unnerving information. I was not sure I could handle all that would need to be done. I did not know how. It seemed as if everything was closing in on me. I could not do anything about it. I was losing control of my body. I came home and cried. This upset Earle immensely. But I needed to cry and get "it" out of my system. Only then could I deal with my situation and do what needed to be done.

Please keep holding my hand, Lord. This is so new to me. Help me!

Dr. Hunt brought in another specialist surgeon, and together with a urologist, they performed the surgery on October 31, 2000. Just have to tell you here that I wrote a few words to Dr. Hunt on a yellow, sticky post-it note. I put that note on my abdomen before I was wheeled into surgery. I asked her to do her best with the gifts that the Holy Spirit had given her. I said something about my possibly having a "gizzard," and not to get it and the colon mixed up. (I was trying to be funny in a not-so-funny situation.) I also told her I was praying for her. She later told me that she kept that note in her billfold for many years. She liked it so much. And, she assured me that I did not have a gizzard – ha.

Dr. Hunt was pleased with the surgery – minimal blood loss. She said everything looked good. I did, however, have to have a permanent colostomy. There simply was not enough good tissue to reconnect the colon after I healed from the surgery. There had been too much radiation damage. The tumor – about eight inches long and two inches wide – was rock hard and embedded in the pelvic floor. They had to chisel it out, but could not get all of it. It would have debilitated me to scrape out any more. Dr. Hunt said the chemotherapy treatments should take care of the rest of it. Of course, all our children – except Gina, who kept in touch by telephone – and my brother Chip and Fran were with Earle and me through all of this. Since all was well with me, Chip and Fran went home the next day, November 1, my sixtieth birthday.

That very same evening, Dr. Hunt came into my hospital room. She looked at Earle and told him to sit down. She came to my bedside and told me she was very sorry. The pathologist's report showed the tumor was malignant. She was very surprised because everything had looked so good in the surgery. But it was *colorectal cancer, an adenocarcinoma, a cancer of the gland, Stage Two, my third cancer!* This cancer was considered Stage Two because of my previous two cancers. The tumor had penetrated into the colon, but not into any of the lymph nodes.

Thank You, Lord, for another successful surgery and this new diagnosis. Hold my hand, Lord.

Dr. Hunt then asked me which oncologist I wanted. The only one I knew was an Obstetrical/Gynecologist (OB/GYN) oncologist. I figured he would not help, because my problem was not in the area of the body he treats. I asked Dr. Hunt to put herself in my place, in that bed. Have a surgeon tell her she had colorectal cancer. Then choose the doctor that she would want for herself.

She told us to wait just a moment and she would be right back. When she returned, she advised us that a Dr. Bassam Mattar would be the one she would want. She had already contacted him. He would be in to see me the next evening, as he would be leaving town the following morning. I was still in shock, as was Earle and everyone else. Gayla immediately put in a call to Chip. He and Fran returned to the hospital right then. When they got to my hospital room, I told him he did not need to come back so quickly. He replied, "Sis, I didn't come back for you, I came back for Earle. I knew you'd be all right." And Earle did need Chip. They were like true brothers, not brothers-in-law.

I cannot remember what I was thinking at that time. It is all hazy. But I do remember trying to deal with a new colostomy. It was hard to see what the nurses were doing as they worked with it. I was still a little sore from the surgery. I was scared to move too much. I was afraid I might break something or pull out something. Dr. Hunt had used the same incision for my colon resection/colostomy surgery that was used for my hysterectomy. So, I only had one scar. But now I had a colostomy too.

Hold my hand, Lord. I need Your help.

The nurse expert who was to show me how this colostomy pouch system worked was on vacation at that time. Her replacement was not very much help. She gave me a video to watch. This was all too new. I had never dealt with anything like this before. I felt almost helpless. As I look back, it really took me years to learn how to deal with a colostomy. But **it is do-able.** Other colostomy patients should be told this. And now, I try to help as many people as I can with all the information I have accumulated. It is like: "Been there and done that. Here's what helped me." Then, maybe others will not have to go through the same adversity I did.

Please hold the hands of all us cancer patients, Lord. We need You.

The next evening Dr. Mattar came to my room and introduced himself. From there began another wonderful doctor/patient/family relationship. I love him too. We all love him. However, we all had much trouble understanding him, with his special different accent. So, we had to listen very intently and sometimes ask him to repeat, which he did gladly – and still does. He had already reviewed my case history. He knew about my previous cancers, surgeries, and radiation treatments. He explained that the normal treatment for colorectal cancer was chemotherapy, radiation, and then chemotherapy again. But since I have already had all the radiation I could have in the pelvic area, I would only have the chemotherapy treatments. He would do all that he could for me. He would stand by me, even through the end of life process – if necessary – until I fired him. He would do his best, but the rest was up to God. I asked him what the prognosis of time was. He replied that he thought that with chemotherapy treatments he could give me a normal life, fifteen to twenty years. He also said that without chemotherapy treatments, it would not be nearly as long, perhaps only two to three years.

There was so much information hitting me at one time. I then told him that I was not sure I wanted to undergo chemotherapy treatments. I would think about it and get back with him. He said he would come see me in the morning. He wanted to know my answer before he left town. Then he left the room. Wow, my family became very vocal. What did I mean not wanting to have chemotherapy treatments? Was it because of what my mother had gone through? What was I thinking? Gayla even asked me if I was thinking about what happened to my mom, which of course I was. But, I also was just simply overwhelmed and confused. Earle was absolutely devastated. **My family** wanted me to take the treatments. I remember thinking and saying something like, "Well, to suffer through all those chemotherapy treatments and then only live for fifteen to twenty years more, that would make me be about … seventy-five or eighty years old. Oh, I guess that really is a normal life span, isn't it?" What a dummy – my blonde roots were showing, I guess. I must have been thinking back when I was thirty-five years old and told I had cervical cancer. Now I'm sixty years old, and living to be seventy-five or eighty would be a normal life span. So… of course, I would have the chemotherapy treatments. I would do all I could to stay alive. My family was much relieved to hear me say that. Earle again stayed with me all night in the hospital, but everyone else went home. My Honey never wanted me to be left alone in the hospital. He always stayed with me. We did not sleep much. At least I did not sleep. But I was so glad Earle was with me.

Hold our hands, Lord.

The next morning, we were up and going before five am. I put on my make-up and fixed my hair. Earle did his stuff too. We did not say much to each other. Before six am Earle was sitting in the chair reading. I was sitting on the side of the bed, lost in my thoughts. Dr. Mattar came in. We were amazed he came there so early. Right away, I apologized to him for being so negative the night before. I told him I just was not thinking clearly. I told him yes, I wanted to take the chemotherapy treatments. I wanted to do all I could to stay alive for as long as I could. He walked over to Earle's side of the room and spoke so clearly, I'll never forget the words he said: "No, you do not need to apologize for what you said. I do not know what your religion is, but I believe in Jesus Christ as my Savior. And, I know that He speaks to His people. Sometimes He says no, do not take the treatments. I am going to call you home. Or, He says yes, take the treatments, and in your case, I think you are an excellent candidate to take the treatments and be healed. I would like to help you. I am glad you will do it." He again said he would do his best, but the healing was up to God. He said he was going out of town right then. His office would schedule my appointment and contact me. He wanted me to heal from the surgery first. The six-month regime of chemotherapy treatments would begin in about a month. When he left, Earle and I looked at each other. We knew we had the right doctor. I was still in shock about the whole cancer thing again, but I slept better that night.

Thank You, Lord, for holding our hands.

The next days and weeks were a blur to me. However, I do remember Earle just looking at me so lovingly and sweetly as I was recuperating at home. He said he wished he could take me out of this place and run away somewhere with me. Then I would not have to face this difficult situation. I told him that the only place we could run away to and be safe would be Heaven, and we will be there someday, together. I also remember that he told me he did not know what he would do if he were told he had cancer. I said he would do the same thing I do. That is to pray, to face it squarely, to do everything the doctors recommend, and to hold onto the Lord's hand like I do.

Oh, dear Lord, help us through this ordeal also, please.

I also remember Earle taking good care of me at home and keeping me laughing. He bought me a little bell to ring/jingle when I needed him. Then he told everyone how he had worn out two pairs of shoes running to answer my jingles – ha. He was so good to me and such fun. When it came time to remove the stitches from my abdomen, Dr. Hunt gave him the tool. She told him he could do it at home. And he did. Of course, when I said, "Ouch," he told me to just hush up and "suck it up." I had to laugh which did not help the pain either. Thinking back, though, I guess it really did help. Being former EMTs, we both knew pretty much what to expect, and, laughing helps healing.

Thank You, Lord, for Earle and his humor. Keep holding our hands.

CHAPTER 7

MY SOUL-MATE HONEY HUBBY

My chemotherapy treatments were to begin Wednesday, December 6, 2000, and continue once a week for six months. However, on Friday evening, December 1, my precious soul-mate Honey Earle called Raymond and asked him about the symptoms of a heart attack. Of course, Raymond reminded Earle that Earle was an EMT and knew what the symptoms were. Raymond must then have asked his dad why he was asking that question. I heard Earle tell him he did not have any pain, he just felt like something was sitting on his chest. Earle had said nothing to me about this. I was so surprised. So, Raymond told him to go to the hospital immediately. Earle would not go. He said that the hospital would just look at him, say there's nothing wrong, and send him back home. So I got upset and called Raymond back. Then Raymond threatened to come and bodily carry Earle to his pickup and take him to the ER, which he could easily do as he is a county fireman/EMT.

Earle very grumpily said okay, he would go. But of course, Earle would not let me drive. He drove us to the ER, parked the pickup, and walked into the ER. I was tagging along behind him. The first test, an Electrocardiogram (EKG) showed that he had not had a heart attack, but the laboratory tests including cardiac enzymes indicated something was wrong, something was going on in his heart. They wanted to keep him overnight for more tests. He was admitted to the hospital.

The hospital had called Dr. Hartwell for a referral to a heart specialist. Dr. Ravi Bajaj entered our lives. He ordered an echo stress test and a heart catheterization test. The test results showed blockages in three coronary arteries. We spent another night in the hospital. Dr. Bajaj explained that people with diabetes, like Earle, are prone to this. These blockages do not occur overnight, rather over twenty to twenty-five years. The body learns to compensate, so the blockages are not noticeable. But, over the last few months, it was becoming noticeable. Medicines do not clear up blockages. They only prevent them from getting worse. Symptoms happen five to ten years after the fact. The pain is angina, not a heart attack.

Lord, this is another puzzling situation. Thank You, Lord, for holding our hands through this also.

Dr. Bajaj did say that diabetics have milder chest pain. The good news was his heart muscle looked good. However, he also said these blocked arteries were not causing his leg pain. That was a separate issue. Dr. Bajaj wanted a heart surgeon to review the tests and visit with us. Earle was given new medicines. Dr. Bajaj

31

told Earle he'd like him to be his guest overnight again. Earle said he would, if Doc would pay for it – ha.

On Monday morning December 4, 2000, the heart surgeon came to Earle's room. He explained that all the arteries in Earle's heart were blocked. Two of the arteries were blocked at seventy percent. Medications would not help. Surgery was needed. Also, the fact that Earle had chest pain while lying down doing nothing was definitely not good. Although the EKGs and telemetry were normal, the blockages could lead to something bad. And before that happens, he should have bypass surgery. The surgeon said Earle was a good candidate for successful surgery: ninety-six percent to ninety-seven percent. Although it was not an emergency, he wanted to do the surgery the next day. My Honey was healthy, even with diabetes and arthritis. But because Honey had wanted to be with me during my chemotherapy treatments that were to begin Wednesday, he was reluctant to have his surgery Tuesday. We prayed and he finally agreed to having his surgery first.

Please hold our hands, Lord. This was so unexpected.

So, surgery – with four or five bypasses – was scheduled for six am Tuesday, December 5. The heart surgeon would do the surgery. Dr. Hartwell, Dr. Bajaj, and Earle's diabetes doctor would consult. It is well to remind myself that all through this ordeal (and the others too), we were praying to our Triune God.

Gracious Triune God, Father, Son, and Holy Spirit, please bless the doctors with guidance, knowledge, skills, strength and courage for a successful surgery. Please also bless Earle with strength, courage, peace, love and healing. Hold all our hands, Lord.

Early the morning of December 6, I kissed my Honey "so long until later", and, I put a post-it note on his chest for the doctors, blessing them. I asked them to be sure and take good care of my Honey. Our adult children, Chip and Fran, some loving friends, and I waited in the Surgical Intensive Care Unit (SICU) family waiting room for over six hours.

Please, Lord, hold all of our hands, including the doctors, and guide them through this surgery.

I should have known that something was wrong when I saw the surgeon come into the room. He spoke to the volunteer receptionist, made eye contact with me, then turned and left the room. A nurse came and escorted us to a private room where the surgeon talked with us. He explained that Earle had come through the heart surgery successfully and had six bypasses, but when they had cut open his chest to do the surgery, they found **his sternum eaten up with cancer.** What a shock that was. At that point, the doctors almost just stopped the surgery and closed him back up, They thought they would just send him home to live out his remaining short life time. But, instead, they consulted an oncologist who said to complete the heart bypasses. He said Earle would need a strong heart to go through the treatment that would be needed. As yet, they were not sure what type of cancer he had: bone, plasma cytoma, multiple myeloma, etc.

Thank You, Lord. Hold our hands, Lord.

I do not remember much else that day. I do remember, though, that I told the doctor and several nurses that **we wanted to be with him when he was told he had cancer.** It was very important for us to help Earle through this. We knew he needed our support. We knew he would be devastated. We were told that Earle was still asleep and would be asleep all night. The doctors would tell Earle tomorrow. So we planned on being there bright and early in the morning to be with him when he was told he had cancer. Forget my first chemotherapy treatment. I needed to be with my Honey.

Oh, please hold our hands, Lord God. This was so unexpected. Help us through this.

Earle was in SICU. We arrived prior to six am on Wednesday, December 6. We were in the waiting room of the SICU. We were waiting for the doors to open at six am, so we could go in and be with him when he was told. Dr. Hartwell walked through, saw us, and came immediately to me with such surprise and sorrow in her eyes. She said she was so sorry and upset to hear that Earle was diagnosed with cancer. She told us when she left the hospital the previous day, she had been told that Earle's heart surgery went fine. He was doing great from that. She did not see us and we did not see her at that time. So, I explained that Earle did not know about the cancer yet. We were waiting to go in and be with him when the doctors told him. She looked directly at me and said, "But he already knows. I just saw him. He's the one who told me."

"WHAT?!" I yelled. I was shocked. Then I was angry. I bolted out of the waiting room and into the SICU. I went directly to Earle, somehow getting through those doors that were not supposed to open until six am. I knew I had to calm down first. When I saw him, he was half sitting up in bed. He looked at me with such dull, despondent, hopeless eyes. I cried – but only on the inside. I could not let him see or hear my tears. His first words to me were, "Do the kids know?" I could not speak. I could only nod my head yes. I went closer to him and tried to hold him. When I could finally talk, I said, "Honey, I am so sorry. We were supposed to be with you when they told you. How did you find out?" Earle replied, "Some doctor I don't even know just showed up at my bedside a little while ago and said, 'Well, you have cancer, but you need to get over your heart surgery first. We'll deal with the cancer later.' And then he left." My Honey was so dejected. I tried so hard not to cry, at least not out loud. I needed to be strong for him and the kids. I knew how this would affect him. I loved him so much – I never wanted to see him hurt. He's my soul-mate Honey.

First me, now Earle…

Please, Lord, hold our whole bodies.

God gave me the strength to compose myself just as Dr. Hartwell and Fran came through the open doors to Earle's bed. Dr. Hartwell knew how mad I was, not at her of course, but at the oncologist who did not honor our request to be with Earle when he was told he had cancer. I even asked the nurse who took care of Earle. She said she never saw that doctor come in or go out.

She said he must have come in the back way. Well, the damage was done. And I mean damage – talk about insensitivity. How could a doctor do that to Earle. We knew how desolate and helpless Earle would feel when he was told. I remembered what he had said to me me earlier, about not knowing what he would do if he were told he had cancer. But now we had to help Earle. We talked and Dr. Hartwell told us we could have whatever doctor we wanted. I told Earle we could fire the oncologist that had told him without us being there. Earle could also have Dr. Mattar, my oncologist, if he wanted, and Earle did want that. He knew and trusted Dr. Mattar as my doctor. He would also trust him as his own doctor. I tried to joke and said, "Honey, we'll be the first husband and wife tag team in chemotherapy." But he wouldn't even smile. We talked a little more. Then we three left so the kids could come in and see their dad, which they did. In the hall outside the SICU, I explained to Dr. Hartwell why I was so angry. Why I did not want that oncology doctor, whom we had never met, anywhere near Earle or me or any of my family members. I know she understood.

Keep holding our hands, Lord. Please don't let go. We need You now more than ever.

Now, I need to tell something here, so you understand where I was coming from in the above situation. After Earle's heart surgery, we had been told that Earle had cancer. It was our understanding that they would tell him the next day with us present. He was in SICU. We could not visit with him again until six am the next day. So we would all go home for the night and get some rest. We would then return early the next morning.

Chip and Fran went home with me. I had trouble going to sleep that night. I was so restless. My mind was trying to comprehend everything all at once. I could not relax or rest. When I finally did fall asleep, I had a dream. In my dream, which was more like a nightmare, some doctor went in to see Earle before we got there. He told Earle that Earle had cancer. When we arrived in the SICU waiting room, this same doctor said he had already told Earle. He said he did not have to wait for us to be with Earle when he told him.

So, I decked him.

Of course, security was called, and that's when I woke up. It was so real and strange. I was so confused and perplexed. Why would I dream something as odd as that? That is not like me. Early the next morning, I told Chip and Fran about this strange dream as Chip was driving us to the hospital. I also told them that what I dreamed better not really happen. Well, it did happen. My dream – nightmare – did come true.

But, thank You, Lord, for holding my hands so that I did not deck the doctor who I didn't even know. And thank You, Lord, for continuing to guide me and help me learn to forgive that doctor. After all, doctors are human and make mistakes also. We need You more than ever now, Lord. Don't let go of our hands.

Earle did very well from the heart surgery. He actually had six bypasses. Earle's blood sugar readings went up for awhile after surgery and we had to deal with that. It is a fact that surgery causes an increase in blood sugar.

The nicest thing happened on Saturday, December 9. Our Pastor Brack and some of the men (Harry, Wendell and Warren) from our church came to the hospital and had their weekly Bible Study in Earle's room. Pastor said that since Earle could not go to them where they met at the church, they would come to him in the hospital. That was great. Earle was so appreciative.

Thank You, Lord, for Pastor Brack and Earle's wonderful friends. Earle needed their presence and their prayers also.

Dr. Mattar, Dr. Hartwell, Dr. Bajaj and the other doctors all took good care of my Honey. Dr. Mattar did a Bone Marrow Aspiration with Biopsy and Chromosome Study on Monday, December 11, 2000. Gary stayed with Earle and me for that biopsy, as it was very painful. Then Earle was released by the hospital to go home. Gary and our friends, Warren and Tammy, helped me get Earle home in the midst of a terrible snow and freezing ice storm. The streets were so very slippery and dangerous. Then began Earle's recuperation.

Thank You, Lord, for doctors, loved ones, and friends.

On Wednesday, December 13, Glynne' took me to my second chemotherapy treatment at the cancer center. The first treatment went fine as planned. Gayla took Earle for his appointment with

Dr. Mattar at the cancer center also. Earle and Gayla came walking through the treatment room where I was. He wanted to see what was happening, how this treatment was being accomplished. Remember, he wanted to be with me during all my chemotherapy treatments. Plus, now he was going to be having these treatments himself. He just looked all around the room. The chairs were full of people taking chemotherapy treatments, with intravenous (IV) tubes infusing the chemicals into their bodies. Then he and Gayla left to go to the waiting room until it was time for his doctor's appointment.

When my treatment was completed, we all went into Dr. Mattar's office. Dr. Mattar explained the results of the various tests. The X-rays had shown questionable – possibly metastatic – areas on Earle's skull and spine. This meant that the cancer may have already spread to these parts of his body. But we knew the spine vacancy was from his laminectomy in 1998, and the spot on his skull only showed on one side. Therefore, it could be just a shadow on the X-ray. We were hopeful. It was determined that **two types of cancer were involved: plasma cytoma and multiple myeloma.** The multiple myeloma was **Stage One**. This meant the cancer had been caught early. We were pleased with this report. We were told the overall survival prognosis for this type cancer is about forty-eight months. More years can be added if the patient is treated with chemotherapy treatments and stem cell transplants. With treatments, more than fifty percent of patients live seven years or longer. Much more information was given us.

Thank You, Lord. We still need You so much.

However, I could tell Earle did not hear it. I was definitely having much trouble concentrating as well. Earle told Dr. Mattar he would do the chemotherapy treatments, but he would not do the stem cell transplants. He said his siblings were much older than him. He would not ask them to supply their stem cells for him. Earle would not even consider having the doctors harvest his own stem cells for future transplanting back into his body. I think Earle felt his own bone marrow was not healthy enough to try that procedure. Dr. Mattar wanted him to heal from the heart surgery first. Then, in four weeks, he would start the chemotherapy treatments. He also wanted to do a Magnetic Resonance Image (MRI) in four weeks. With all that information swirling around in our heads, we started for home. Glynne' took me and Gayla took Earle, but Earle wanted to run an errand first. They did and then Gayla took him to lunch. The next day, one of the kids stayed with Earle, while Gayla took me to one-day surgery. Dr. Hunt, my colon surgeon, placed a portable catheter (port-a-cath) in my upper right chest. This would be used for the IV infusion of the chemicals for the treatments. The veins in our chests are larger than the veins in our arms, therefore, there is less damage to the veins via a port-a-cath. I was so glad to get it. It is such a wonderful invention, but a good surgeon has to insert it.

Keep holding our hands, Lord.

It was Friday, December 15, 2000. It was the first time in weeks, though it seemed like months, that Earle and I were alone at home. We enjoyed this time so much and reminisced about so many different things. We knew it was not going to be easy, but Earle wanted to do everything the doctors told him was important, and he did. He was doing just what we had previously talked about: pray, stand up against the cancer and do everything the doctors told him. And, holding onto the Lord's hand was so important. I was so proud of him. We just spent time with each other, not even talking at times. We were close to each other, enjoying each other, just living life. Earle was very apprehensive about his chest after this heart surgery. He held that red heart-shaped pillow that the hospital gave him – as they give all heart surgery patients – against his chest all the time. It helped so much when he had to cough. He also worried about getting his chest bumped during the night. So, to ease his discomfort, I slept in the guest room that night.

Comfort Earle and hold his hand, Lord.

CHAPTER 8

BREATH OF ETERNAL LIFE

Very early in the morning of Saturday, December 16, Earle called me to come help him. His left leg was bleeding slightly in a few places from the incision where they had taken veins to put in his heart for the six bypasses. A mammary artery had also been used. Earle's incision went from his left groin down the inside of his leg to almost his ankle. I cleaned the incision where needed and put on more sterile-strips the hospital had given us. I placed a call in to the doctor. The on-call doctor returned my call and told me what to do. I had already done what he said to do. Then Earle told me that he had gotten up during the night. He had walked twenty-two times around the kitchen, living room, and halls in our home – almost like a circle. The doctor had told him to walk. That is what he was doing. He was very determined to follow all the doctor's instructions.

I fixed a good breakfast for Earle and we ate. He was agitated for some reason. I tried to figure out how I could help him. He also was very upset over all the medications he was having to take. I had prepared a computerized list of all his medications, with prescription numbers, dosages, dates, etc. This list had the doctors' names and why each medicine was prescribed. I thought it might help him to see the need for the various medications. Then, he could fill his pill container with all these medications. That way he could have more control over his situation. He did that while I was in the office paying some bills or something. When I checked back on him, he was wanting to move to the living room and read his Bible. I carried a fresh cup of coffee to him. He sat in the blue rocking chair with his Bible to read. I went back into the office. Everything seemed okay.

Hold his hand, Lord.

The telephone rang. It was Gina checking on her dad. I brought her up to date on what was going on with him. Then her sweet daughter, Tarah, wanted to talk. I talked with her a few minutes. Then I told Tarah she needed to talk to her grampa also. I took the phone to Earle. I returned to the office. In a few minutes, I heard Earle very abruptly say, "Tarah, I gotta go. Bye." That was so unusual for him. I hurried into the living room wondering if Tarah had said something to upset him. This seemed very unlikely, as he loved his children and grandchildren so much. I asked Earle what was wrong, what happened? Did Tarah say something to upset him? He just looked at me and said, "I don't know, but I'm having trouble breathing." Then, I remembered the doctors told us this might happen. So, I reminded him of this. I told him to try to relax, take as deep a breath as possible, and the feeling should go away. I held on to him and hugged him.

Hold our hands, Lord. Help him to breathe, Lord.

He stood up. I asked where he was going. He said, "I don't know, but I'm getting dizzy." I helped him over to the couch to lie down. I did not want him to fall. His breathing was difficult and sparse. My EMT training began to kick in. I asked him if he was hurting. Did his chest, neck, back, arms hurt? And he said, "No, ….I…. just….can't ….breathe..." I told him I was going to call the doctor again. He shook his head yes. I called the doctor again and was put on hold. I tried to get Earle's vital signs. I could not even get his pulse. He asked me to pray for him, which I did. I remember asking God to give Earle His breath of life. I truly meant for God to give my Honey His earthly breath of life. But God had other plans for my precious soul-mate Honey, hubby.

I then told Earle I could not wait any longer for the on-call doctor to answer. I was going to hang up and call the ambulance. Earle nodded yes. I called 9-1-1 immediately. Then I called our son Raymond. It was only about 8:45am. I was still in my nightgown. I told Earle I had to quickly put on some clothes to unlock the door for the emergency personnel. He did not want to let go of my hand. He again asked me to pray, which I did. He asked me to hurry, which I did. I kept asking Earle if he had any pain. He would reply, "No,...I....just….can't....breathe!"

The tears are filling my eyes as I recall what happened next. This is so difficult, Lord. Hold our hands, please, Lord.

Earle wanted me near him, holding his hand, which I was. In between his gasps for breaths, he said he had to go to the bathroom. I was afraid I couldn't handle him by myself, so I told him to hold on until help arrived. Earle said something about what could they do? Then, his eyes started to roll back and I almost panicked. I told him to hold on and that I loved him. The city/county fire department volunteers arrived first. They immediately put oxygen on Earle. Raymond came in right behind them.

Volunteer Melvin just stepped back and said, "What do you want us to do, Ray?"

Raymond looked at me with eyes of such unbelief that this could be happening to his own father. He said, "Mom, we've got to get Dad on the floor! Pray, Mom!" So, he and I moved Earle to the floor, and I prayed. Raymond's EMT training served him well. He requested other medical equipment which they gave him. He began questioning his dad, who again struggled to tell us that he did not hurt, he just could not breathe. Earle's eyes rolled back again.

Raymond said, "Dad, hold on, we can beat this cancer! Don't give up, try to breathe, Dad! Please just take one big breath for me, Dad!" And Earle tried so hard to breathe. He was gasping for a breath of air, but he could not get any. Raymond could see the panicked look in his father's eyes as he struggled to breathe.

Earle's eyes began to roll back again. Raymond realized Earle needed Cardio Pulmonary Resuscitation (CPR), but he could not do CPR on his own dad.

Hold Raymond's hands, Lord.

Melvin told Raymond to do what he had to do. So, Raymond started CPR. I know how much it hurt Raymond to do CPR on his own father. But he knew he had to. *I was holding Earle's hand, praying. Raymond was doing CPR. We watched the life leave Earle's eyes as he transitioned to Heaven! I was astounded! Earle was now in the arms of Jesus!*

Hold our hands, Lord. I kept praying. Hold us all close to You, Lord. Don't let go of us.

The ambulance crew and paramedics arrived. A police officer and I do not know who else also arrived. The paramedics did what they were supposed to do. But I knew it was already too late. And all through this bewildering experience, I felt like I was being cradled, held close in the arms of my Lord and Savior. I felt everything was going to be okay, and Earle was okay. And the song, "Heaven Came Down and Glory Filled My Soul," kept running through my mind. I kept praying. I told Earle I would see him in Heaven. **There was a strange peace surrounding me, a peace that passes all understanding.**

I don't remember what I said or did then. I do remember a police officer telling us he would contact Adam, our good friend on the county sheriff's department. I remember Raymond telling me to ride in the ambulance with Dad. He would tell the rest of the kids and then they would come to the hospital. I rode up front in the ambulance with Beth, our good friend and a volunteer with the city/county Emergency Medical Service (EMS). I remember telling her that Earle was already in Heaven. I told her that no matter what they did or how hard they tried, they could not bring him back. I also knew that when we arrived at the hospital ER, they would take Earle away from me. I would not see him again. I was now without him here on earth. I knew in my heart that he was already with our Savior. Yet, I felt so different and perplexed, like this was all only a dream.

Is this really happening? Hold our hands, Lord.

I do not know how it is possible to think or be in two different places at the same time. But I remember being on the verge of panic. I was ready to go completely out of control. Yet I was full of peace. One part of me wanted to scream, **"No, No, No! It can't be! He's not dead!"** But another part of me was calm, **accepting the fact that Earle's earthly life was over. He had gone on to Heaven.** I would never see him or talk to him again here on earth. It was such a strange feeling. It was different from any feeling I had before. There was anger and peace, both at once, fighting for control over me.

Help me, Lord. Keep holding my hand, Lord. Is this how You felt when Your Son gave His life for us?

I was comforted knowing that Earle's last breath on earth was followed immediately by his first breath in Heaven. I felt a submission <u>to</u> the Lord accepting what He had done for Earle. And I felt a peace <u>from</u> the Lord also accepting what He had done for Earle.

Always help me and hold my hand, Lord, just like You held Earle's.

At that point, I was lost. I did not know what to do. I guess I did what they told me to do. When we arrived at the ER, so many people were already there waiting for us. Raymond's entire county fire department crew from his station was there, including Captain Davey and Lieutenant Kip. Of course, our friend Adam arrived. Our County Sheriff Stan and his wife also came. I think our pastor and several friends from church arrived. More firemen and policemen were there. Many friends of our children came also to support us. I cannot begin to name them all. How blessed we are.

Thank You, Lord, for all our friends and loved ones.

The ER trauma doctor came to tell me, and all of us, that they could not do anything to save Earle. He was gone. I told him I knew that already, but I wanted to know what had happened that actually took Earle's life. I had thought that maybe his stitches from the bypass surgery had come loose from all his walking during the night and he bled to death. This would have been **before** any CPR was done. Earle had told us he did not have any pain. He just could not breathe. The doctor told us apparently several small blood clots broke loose and were blocking Earle's lungs. That made it difficult for him to breathe.

Then, one huge blood clot broke loose and completely blocked his lungs. He could not breathe at all then and he died. The doctor also stated Earle probably had no pain during his struggle to breathe. That made sense knowing what Earle had kept telling us. The doctor also said having both the heart surgery and the multiple myeloma cancer had quadrupled Earle's chances of getting blood clots. We all know that blood clots are always a risk in any type surgery.

I choose to believe that it was the Lord's will this had happened. He took Earle home to Heaven, so that Earle would not have to suffer through the treatments and a less-than-good prognosis. This was God's plan for Earle's life. Earle had accomplished what God wanted him to do. Now Earle could rest. At least he did not hurt anymore or have to struggle and gasp for breath.

Thank You, Lord, for Earle and for holding his hand while You took him home with You.

I truly believe that the Holy Spirit was with all of us that December morning. He held us all up, as He separated us, knowing that we would some day be together again. I tried to be so strong for the kids, especially Raymond. He had tried so hard to save his dad. I am so proud of him for trying. It took incredible courage. I know he has suffered from this. I want him and all my children to know that God has plans for each of us. No matter what we do or do not do, God will fulfill His plans. We should not be discouraged when God's plans do not result in what we think they should. We should ask God to help us understand, to just accept, and to learn from what He planned and fulfilled. We know that our Triune God is in control. He not only knows what happens to each of us, but He has allowed it to happen. He wants us to learn to trust in Him. He wants us to lean on Him, to give Him our burdens, to obey Him, and to love Him. We must remember: Everything in life is according to God's will, not our will.

Keep holding my children's hands, Lord. Thank You for the blessing of all of them.

When the ER chaplain asked me how long Earle and I had been married, I replied, "Just thirty-two years." He said something like, "Just thirty-two years. That's a long time." I told him yes it is, but I wanted another thirty-two years with Earle. I was not yet ready to give him up. The ER trauma doctor told us we could go in the room to see Earle then. Our family went in to Earle, prayed and said our goodbyes. I was still numb. Again, I felt I was in a dream. Earle looked so peaceful, like he was just sleeping. He was not hurting at all, but he was not breathing either. I kept hoping they were wrong. I kept hoping this was truly just a dream. I wanted and waited for him to open his eyes and start breathing again and talk to me. But, he didn't. I had lost him here on earth.

Now I'm lost too.

Hold our hands, Lord.

Chapter 9

Going Home to Heaven

Have you ever lost a spouse or other loved one? I know now why they say the word "lost." You cannot find them. You cannot talk to them. You cannot hear them. You cannot see them. You cannot be with them. You cannot touch them. They are lost. And you know what? So are you. At least, I was lost. It was so difficult to get through the next days. There's so much I do not remember. And yet, some things I do remember very clearly.

While we were still in the ER waiting room, one of my kids called Gina, who lived out of state. She was told what had happened to her dad. I was still in a state of shock, not fully aware of everything going on around me. The ER staff started asking questions. Even though the questions were standard and necessary, I considered them horrible. First. we had to immediately select a funeral home to use. I wasn't ready for this.

Decisions for all the other questions had to also be made before we could even go home.

At least all of us but Earle could go home.

Time passed so quickly and yet so slowly. It was time to go home. I was to go home without Earle to an empty house that would never be the same again, to our bed all by myself. I would never have his arms around me again, never enjoy being with him again, never laugh with him again, never even talk with him again. I would never love with him again. It was time to go home. Alone. And yet, there was a calm peace surrounding me that kept me from going hysterical. I knew I was not alone and never would be.

Thank You, my Lord and Savior, for holding me up.

The only things I remember during the next few days were the preparations for the funeral. Many, many friends came by and offered their sympathy and gifts. There was this strange peace that held me up. My wonderful children and their families were so helpful. I could not have made it through this as easily without them. Survival instincts then kicked in. We started making all the arrangements, things had to get done. Gina and her family already had reservations to come home for Christmas the next Wednesday. We decided to wait and hold the funeral on the Thursday after they arrived.

Thank You, Lord, for my fantastic family. Hold their hands too, Lord.

Since we had not chosen a local funeral home, I realized it would be difficult for friends to view Earle prior to the funeral. The visitation was planned for Wednesday, December 20, 2000, in our church's fellowship hall. The funeral was scheduled for Thursday, the next day, in our church as well. Raymond questioned me about the amount of room we would need for all the people who would likely attend. He did not think our church was big enough. He was right, as we later learned.

Thank You, Lord.

We were blessed with a very nice happening. Our church friends, Warren and Tammy, in their great kindness, offered to make arrangements with the funeral home to allow Earle's body to remain in the fellowship hall Wednesday night after the visitation until the service the next day. Warren and Tammy then organized our fellow members to have someone stay with Earle the entire night until he was taken to the church the next day for the funeral. That was so precious to our family. I will be eternally grateful to all our friends for doing this for us.

Please bless all our precious friends, Lord.

Despite the bitter cold and icy conditions, visitors came in droves to pay their respects. These visitors included the sheriff's officers, policemen, firemen, doctors, pastors, and a great number of family and friends from everywhere. There were even friends from our past whom we had not heard from in years. Our church members and friends provided food for everyone. Since I had my third chemotherapy treatment that morning, Fran and my kids were keeping close tabs on me. They tried to protect me from getting bumped on my port-a-cath while getting hugs from everyone. It was a series of firsts for me. First funeral of a soul-mate. First time going through chemotherapy treatments. First time to let my children take over the organizing and run the show. First time to be alone at home. It was also the first time for me to really **wonder about my future, or if I would even have a future.**

Thank You, Lord, for holding our hands through all of this.

The morning of the funeral was starkly beautiful. The sun shone bright through the biting cold and damp, bone-chilling wind. Yet, I was numb to it. I tried desperately to stay calm and not lose control of myself and my emotions. I had to be strong for my kids, our family, and all Earle's and my friends. I knew that I had to keep control. If I ever let go, I would never return to normal again. I would be lost in a major mental breakdown, and I could not let that happen. God would not let that happen. Earle would not want that to happen. He always looked to me to be the strong one.

Help me, Lord, keep holding my hand.

Each of our sons and daughters had a spouse or very close friend to help them through this ordeal. I was so grateful. Chip and Fran were at my side to help me also.

Thank You, Lord God Almighty, for holding all of us close to You.

There were so many people at the funeral. Raymond was right about the space. We did not have enough room inside the church. All of the pews were full. The extra chairs that were set up were full also. People had to stand inside the church, in the narthex, and outside the church in the bitter cold. The sheriff's department, firemen, policemen, other law enforcement officers, and so many friends and family were there. I cannot remember all of them.

Thank You, Lord, for Pastor Brack and his wonderful uplifting message. He is also with You now, Lord. Thank You also, Lord, for all these friends and families.

The bagpiper played "Amazing Grace" as he led the procession out of the church. I followed Earle's casket, holding onto the arm of Michael's little son. I had to look up to keep from looking people in the eye. I had to focus on my Lord and Savior to help me through this. I hurt so much. I wanted to run away, but where would I go? I know the tears were streaming down my face as I continued to look up. But I had to hold my head up and get through this. I listened as the last sounds of the bagpipe whispered away into oblivion, and I knew it was final.

Lord, I desperately need Your help. Please don't let go of my hand.

I do remember Raymond's fire truck led the procession. It was followed by sheriff's and police cars, and more fire trucks, all the way from the church to the cemetery in our home town. It was an awesome sight. At each major intersection along that drive, there was a law enforcement or a fire vehicle to block the road for us. I was overwhelmed at this turn out for Earle. I had no idea how respected and loved he was by so many people. I knew I loved him and so did our kids, but to see this honor given to him by so many others was a surprise. I was shocked. I was so grateful to all of them for showing this respect for him.

Bless them also, Lord.

At the cemetery, there was a strange and wonderful occurrence. I felt it was a "coincidence" from our Lord. While a veteran was playing taps, some planes flew over us. Earle was a former U.S. Marine. He had been a pilot before I met him. A train went by and whistled. Earle had worked for the Rock Island Railroad for twenty-one plus years. The sheriff presented me the U.S. flag that his officers had ceremoniously folded. Earle had retired as undersheriff. It was as though our Lord was telling us that Earle had lived a full life. He was loved and respected by many, and our Lord was welcoming Earle home and saying, ***"Well done, thou good and faithful servant; enter thou into the joy of the Lord!"*** **(Matthew 25:21)** And there was that strange peace enveloping me again.

Thank You, Lord, for holding our hands and for loaning us Earle for so many years. Thank You, Lord, for taking Earle home to his rest with You.

All through the time of Earle's death and burial, it seemed as if our Lord would not let me panic. Two songs kept running through my mind, "Heaven Came Down and Glory Filled My Soul" and "Jesus, Jesus, Jesus, Sweetest Name I Know." This is the gospel song we had sung at the dedication of our new church building. Earle had played the guitar and we both sang. I could not shake either of these beautiful songs. Now I am so glad for them. They kept me sane during an insane time.

Thank You, Lord, for the gifts of music and Your Word.

CHAPTER 10

LIFE AND DEATH CONTINUE

My lovely children took turns taking me to my chemotherapy treatments to complete the six-month treatment plan. I am so grateful they did this for me. They wanted to help me because they knew their father had planned to be there for me. However, I had a bad attitude or else I was grieving for Earle. I do not know which, maybe both. I just know that life was emotionally rough on me during this time. I am sure it was on the kids also, but they never complained or said anything.

Thank You, Lord, for these wonderful children.

At the completion of this round of chemotherapy treatments, **my third cancer was in remission.** This remission lasted for one year and one month.

Thank You for holding my hand through this, Lord. Thank You also, Lord, for holding the hands of my precious children and their families.

I then asked Dr. Hunt to remove the port-a-cath. The cancer was in remission. As far as I was concerned, I was through with it. Neither she nor Dr. Mattar wanted to remove it at this time. I found out later they had better insight into the future than I did. Dr. Hunt did go ahead and remove it, though. She let me keep it as an example – after she cleaned it up, of course. Now when I am speaking to a group, I show it to those who might benefit from having a port-a-cath.

Thank You, Lord, for these wonderful doctors.

On June 2, 2001, a terrible event for our family happened. Our daughter, Gina, was almost killed by electrocution. As Raymond stated, it was a good thing Earle was already in Heaven. This would have been too much for him. First Gayla, now Gina. Our entire family suffered through this. There is not enough room to tell her story here. Gina is going to write about it someday. I'll let her do just that. It's her story and a good one. Suffice it to say that two years later on June 2, 2003, our good Lord healed Gina completely. She is in perfect health today. Now, she can and does share her story with others.

Thank You, Lord, for holding our hands through this also. Thank You for keeping our family together again. Thank You for teaching us how to share You and Your Word with others.

In May 2001, another happy event occurred. A new great-grandson, Grant, was born to Josh and his wife.

Thank You, Lord, for yet another baby to love.

Another wonderful happening took place in 2001. Raymond and Jennifer were married on the same day as my parent's wedding anniversary. This happy event added three more grandchildren: Oliver, Libby, and Cole. How fascinating and blessed it is to know that Raymond followed in his dad's footsteps. He, too, married a woman with children that he could help raise.

Life is good, Lord, thank You.

On June 17, 2002, the day after Father's Day, God called my father home to Heaven with Him. In August of 2001, Chip and Fran and I had transferred Dad from the nursing home in Chip's town to the nursing home in my town. Dad had thought he should be able to come home with me instead. We explained to Dad that if he were with me, he would get to see only me. It would wear out both of us. We had to consider that I had very little energy left because of all the chemotherapy treatments, and the nursing home had social experiences that he would not get at my house or Chip's. Plus, the caretakers worked in eight-hour shifts, not twenty-four hours like I would have to work. They would be fresh and ready to care for him properly as he should be cared for. He finally accepted this. At one point he told me, "Daughter, I have learned to be content in whatever situation I am in." I was so glad to hear him quote Scripture.

Thank You, Lord, for my father and his faith.

The good Lord knew what was in the future, but we did not. As it turned out later, I had to go back into treatment again. Therefore, I would have been unable to properly care for Dad.

I visited Dad several times a week. Raymond and Jennifer took him to their home in the country for a meal several times. He loved that. In the nursing home, Dad became ill, with pneumonia, and was taken to a local hospital. Chip and Fran drove down and stayed with me so they could also visit him. We celebrated Father's Day with him in the hospital. Several of our cousins also came to visit Dad that day: Dolores and Charles, LaVada and Carl, Jerry and Melba, Leroy and Marilyn, and Billy and Joan. Dad was pleased to see all of them. He was the only uncle they had left. When everyone left the hospital, I prayed with Dad as I always did. I told him I would see him the next morning. Dad kept rubbing his chest and saying, "Godfrey, it hurts." We thought it was the pneumonia and asked the nurses for pain medication. They gave him Tylenol.

The next morning, Chip and Fran left before me to go to the hospital. We were driving separately because they would be going back to their home from the hospital. Jennifer called me and asked me to wait for Raymond. He wanted to go with me. I was in a hurry and did not want to wait. I thought he could drive himself and meet us there, but Jennifer insisted I wait. So, I did. I was just getting ready to leave when Raymond drove up. He told me, "Mom, Grampa's gone."

I was in a daze. I did not understand or comprehend what he was telling me. When the news finally sunk in, I was devastated. I had just seen Dad last night. He was going to be all right. How could this be? We found out Dad had died that morning just before Chip and Fran got to the hospital. They called Raymond to have him come tell me. That's why Raymond took me to the hospital. We made the final arrangements for Dad that he wanted. He did not want a funeral like I wanted to have for him. He only wanted a graveside service and to be buried in the cemetery next to Mom. I had wanted to have a funeral for Dad like we had for Mom. Chip asked me, "Sis, what did Dad tell you he wanted?" I had to admit he only wanted a graveside service. So, that is what we gave him. Lots of people came to pay their respects for him.

Thank You, Lord, for the blessing of my mom and dad and for their faith, quiet as it was.

CHAPTER 11

MY FIRST RECURRENCE OF CANCER

Then in July 2002, the results of regularly scheduled tests showed that the spot/area/tumor had started growing again in my pelvic area. This was the **first recurrence of colorectal cancer, now Stage Four**. This was not good. It was diagnosed as Stage Four because it was a recurrence of the third type of cancer. This was my fourth attack of cancer.

A new treatment plan to fight this cancer began. Again, my children took me to chemotherapy treatments for another six months. Every other week two chemicals were infused. I also wore a "chemo pump" for forty-eight hours. At that time, Gary was on second shift. He would take me in the morning. Then Glynne' would join us around noon. We would usually have lunch together in the treatment room. Gary would then go to work. At the completion of my treatment, Glynne' would take me home. It was wonderful to share time with my children. The nurses all loved my children and looked forward to their coming to be with me. Of course, I had to ask Dr. Hunt to insert a new port-a-cath for the chemotherapy treatments. Remember, I had her remove the first one, which I kept to show others.

This second round of chemotherapy treatments made me think about what was truly happening to me. I realized it had been nearly eighteen months that I had been without Earle. I had also survived this cancer that long. Consequently, I had an "attitude adjustment." I remembered what Earle had told me years ago: look forward to the good results at the end of the treatment. I knew I was going to spend several hours in the chair with the IV infusing. Therefore, I felt I should use that time wisely. I made a prayer journal and started praying for people. I remember once, I was bent over in the chair praying quietly. A nurse stopped and said, "Oh, Hon, don't sleep like that. Please sit up and be more comfortable." I told her that I was not sleeping, I was praying. I had to laugh to myself over that one – but how sweet and thoughtful of her. I had wonderful care by all the nurses.

"Thank You for these skilled, caring, and dedicated nurses, Lord.

Six more months of chemotherapy treatments were completed. **This first recurrence of cancer was in remission. This was the second attack of colorectal cancer.** This remission lasted two years and seven months.

Thank You, Lord, for holding my hand and the hands of my children.

In February of 2003, our Hensley family welcomed another member. My twelfth grandchild, Samuel, first-born son of Raymond and Jennifer, came into this world with great gusto. He yelled, not cried, for thirty minutes. I had driven Jennifer and Oliver to the hospital. Raymond, who was on duty, was waiting for us. I will let Jennifer or Oliver tell you about the trip to the hospital. Funny, but two years later, when Jack was born, Jennifer would not let me drive her to the hospital. Oh well.

Thank You, Lord, for another beautiful gift of life to love.

The chemotherapy treatment plan for this first recurrence of colorectal cancer had included two chemicals. One of the chemicals caused neuropathy in my feet, toes, hands, and fingers. The chemicals also affected my balance. It is true that there is a problem called "chemo brain". Some of the chemicals cause short-term memory loss. They also affect your ability to concentrate and to comprehend. Many people agree with this "chemo brain" definition – just ask a cancer survivor of chemotherapy treatments. However, I must note here that in my case, I was blessed with the ability to read, concentrate and study my Bible. Isn't God great! I could not read any other books, but I could read and study God's Word.

To counteract some of the bad side effects of the chemotherapy treatments, I started taking senior citizen tap-dancing classes. I did not tell my children I was doing this. I just told them I was going to exercise. These classes helped me regain some of my balance. The classes also helped strengthen my feet and ankles.

They also worked on improving my memory. I had to really concentrate to learn each dance. Of course, it was fun for me.

We had our family Christmas celebration, December 28, 2003, in my home. I decided to surprise my family with the results of all my hard work. I told them to wait downstairs in the family room in front of the television. I found out later they thought I had produced a video, but I had not. However, producing a video is a great idea that I should probably pursue. You can imagine their surprise when I carried in a four foot by four foot sheet of heavy plywood. I put it on the floor in front of the television. I started the music and took off my robe. I had used the robe to cover up my dance costume. Then I did my little tap-dance, complete with hat and cane.

Now you should know that any child taking tap-dancing lessons could do better than I did. But, I did it anyway. I wanted to show my family that I had not given up on life and its challenges. When the short dance was over, I told them through my tears that there was no way I could repay them for all that they had done for me. They had helped me through their father's death. They had supported me through these two bouts with colorectal cancer. I wanted to show them the "gift of life." I wanted them to know I was going to be okay now. I was getting on with my life. I wanted them to do that also. I wanted them to enjoy life every day. I wanted them to see how the Lord had held me up through all of this. I wanted them to know that our Lord would hold them up also. The grandchildren were the most vocal over my dance. James said, "Gramma, that was awesome!" Gina said she wished she would have known what I was going to do. She would have videotaped it – ha. That is exactly why I did not tell them ahead of time. We had a great family celebration.

Thank You, Lord, for the gift of life.

Again, life was good and back to normal, if there is a normal. My precious children were prospering in life. Grandchildren and great-grandchildren were growing. There were many school events, birthday parties, new church, friends, volunteering, etc. All these activities kept me busy and enjoying life.

CHAPTER 12

MY SECOND RECURRENCE OF CANCER

In January 2005, Raymond and Jennifer had their second son, Jack, my thirteenth grandchild. Then, in February 2005, Joshua, Jr., my fifth great-grandson, was born to Josh and his wife. I was blessed with a grandson and a great-grandson in the same year.

Thank You, Lord, for again blessing us with these beautiful gifts of life to raise Your way.

Dr. Mattar followed my case closely with regular testing. I am so glad he did. He still does. In August 2005, I was told the tumor was growing again in that same spot. This was after two years and seven months of remission. This was the third attack of cancer in that same spot. It was my **second recurrence of colorectal cancer, my fifth attack of cancer. It was Stage Four.**

There was no prognosis. I had already lived longer than they thought I would. But, as Dr. Mattar stated, "I can tell you what the scientific data shows. I do not know what God has planned for you." This time I completed seven months of chemotherapy treatments. These treatments were much rougher than the previous two rounds of treatments. I was beginning to feel even more effects of peripheral neuropathy in my feet, legs, hands and fingers. This was to be expected. The same two chemicals were used in these treatments, plus a new medicine called Avastin. The Avastin zeroed in on the tumor and cut off its blood supply. Without nutrients, the tumor should die. However, there were possible bad side effects caused by this new medicine. One side effect was affecting or altering blood and heart functions. That meant I had to have cardiac tests as well. Those tests showed my heart to be normal. Dr. Mattar had wanted to do a full year of chemotherapy treatments. However, after seven months, all the tests had shown improvement, so I begged him to let me stop taking the treatments. He agreed and gave me a rest from the chemotherapy treatments.

Thank You, Lord, for holding our hands. I praise You for always answering our prayers.

At the same time, Dr. Mattar was trying very hard to deal with some of the side effects of the chemotherapy treatments. The neuropathy in my feet and legs was still there. My hands and fingers were better. He prescribed a different medicine for me that he thought would help. He is such a good doctor. I started taking the medicine on Friday, January 27, 2006. I was so incredibly tired. I could hardly get out of bed to go to the bathroom. On Saturday morning, Raymond borrowed my pickup. When he brought it back, I was still in bed. He told me I did not look good. He said maybe he should call the doctor. Of course, I said no, I just needed some rest. I was so very tired. He fixed me up with some water right by my bedside and told me to drink it. The funny thing is, I thought I did drink it. I remember reaching for it several times, but then I could not remember actually drinking it. And, I do not remember how much of that new medicine I took.

All during this time, a thought kept running through my mind. I was going to be okay. I just needed to rest. I had no energy. I had no fear. I had no comprehension of my severe condition. Several times I remember trying to sit up on the side of the bed. I felt something cold and damp on my side and under me. I do not remember actually sitting up or moving. I was so cold and unbelievably tired. I kept reaching for the covers, but I could not get the covers over me. I knew I had to go to the bathroom. I was afraid my colostomy pouch was full. But I knew I was weak. I did not want to fall. So, I thought about crawling to the bathroom and back. Whether or not I actually did that, I do not know. Gayla said later she thought I must have. I was so extremely tired. I kept trying to get up, but could not. I have never had a sensation like that before. Early Sunday morning, Raymond came back to check on me. I'm so glad he did.

Thank You, Lord, for my heroic and concerned son, Raymond.

Raymond called to me from my front door. I was still in bed. I tried to answer him, but no words would come out. When he came to my bedroom and found me still in bed, he called to me. He said I opened my eyes and replied, "Hi, Sweetie," then I closed my eyes again. He could tell I had not drunk any of the water he had fixed for me the day before. Everything was just as he left it Saturday afternoon. He kept asking me something, but I could not answer him. He had called Gayla and told her the situation. She drove so fast to my house. I think the Holy Spirit actually spirited her there. I think she told him to go ahead and call the doctor. I guess I was still telling him not to call the doctor. Raymond fell back on his career training. He called the doctor and the ambulance.

I remember hearing Raymond say, "She is unresponsive." Now….how could I hear him say that and yet not be able to respond? He continued to say, "She appears to be dehydrated. She is a cancer patient. I've been trying to get vitals, but cannot. She's semiconscious. Every time I try to sit her up, she passes out." Of all that he said, the one thing I hated to hear him say was that I was a cancer patient. I hated cancer. And how could I be dehydrated? I thought I had been drinking water. I was a mess.

Gayla kept telling me that she needed to cut my nightgown off me. She also said for me not to worry because she would buy me a new one. She figured it was my favorite. I remember giggling and saying, at least I think I was saying, "It's all right, go ahead." I never even realized when she did cut it off. I was told afterwards that I kept passing out. Whenever they tried to sit me up or move me, I passed out. That is why I could not remember everything.

Thank You, Lord, for Raymond and Gayla.

When the volunteer fire department arrived, I remember seeing Melvin. He said, "Hi, Gwen." I think I answered him. At least in my mind, I said Hi to him. I remember seeing Gary come to the bedroom door and turn away. Also a policeman came and turned away. Why does everybody have to see me like this? And, how can I be unresponsive and still know some of what is going on? When the ambulance crew got there, the only thing I remember is the cold backboard. And, it was cold outside when they transferred me to the ambulance.

The paramedic, Shawn, kept apologizing to me about sticking me so many times to get an IV started. I kept telling him – at least in my mind I thought I was telling him – it was okay. I knew by then I was really dehydrated. It would be hard for him to find a vein. I remember being so sad to realize my veins were collapsed. I usually drank a lot of water and other fluids. I had read that it was important to drink one ounce of water for every two pounds of your weight. I tried very hard to follow that advice and stay hydrated. In fact, one time a doctor told me he thought maybe I was drinking too much water. I could cut back. But, as Dr. Mattar later told us, it was a combination of several things that caused me to have to go to the hospital. The chemotherapy treatments, my not drinking enough fluids, the new medicine I had taken, vomiting, diarrhea, and my weakened condition all caused me to become dehydrated.

Thank You, Lord, for my family and all these medical helpers.

Raymond and Gary stayed at my house and cleaned up my mess. Gayla followed the ambulance to the hospital. Glynne' met us there. They had called Gina. She started on her way from another town. On the ambulance ride to the hospital, the paramedic finally got an IV started. He was pushing in the fluids. We were almost to the hospital before he could get my blood pressure, which was only seventy over forty. This is very low. I was in and out of consciousness most of the time. There are blank spots in my memory. At the ER, there were several faces I did not recognize, the doctors and nurses and others.

I thank You, Lord, for my sons, Gary and Raymond, for cleaning. Thank You also, Lord, that my daughters, Gayla and Glynne' and later Gina, were with me in the ER. I knew I would be all right.

There was a doctor who wanted to call in a liver specialist, because the lab report showed my liver count was very high. I was trying to tell them no, a liver specialist was not necessary. Gayla had the foresight to bring my cancer book from home. In my book, I keep a record of all my information from all my doctors' appointments, laboratory reports, test reports, etc. I take this book with me every time I have a medical appointment. I kept trying to tell the ER doctors to check my lab reports in my book. They would see that two weeks ago my liver count was fine and normal. It had to be this dehydration that had caused the high count. I did not need a specialist. All I needed was some rest. I was so extraordinarily tired. I would try to answer questions or make comments. But I am not sure the words came out. I was still in and out of consciousness.

Thank You, Lord, for Gayla. She had brought my book and could find and show the medical personnel the information they needed to verify my condition.

I do remember a doctor asking me if I had a Do Not Resuscitate (DNR) order or a living will. I was trying to say yes, but I wanted to live. I did not want to die. Since I wasn't fully conscious and could not answer all their questions, I was afraid they might decide right then to just let me die. One of my girls kept talking to me to keep me awake. This helped me so much. I tried to say to this doctor to read the papers. They would state that two doctors needed to determine that I was brain dead, in order to let me die, but the words would not come out right. **I certainly was not brain dead. My brain was working, but my mouth was not working.** My daughters helped me greatly. They told the doctor what I was trying to say.

Thank You, Lord, for my quick-thinking daughters.

I was becoming angry that the doctor would even think such a thing. This made me wonder what would happen to someone who did not have family with them? Somewhere in here I saw my sons come to the door to see me. Then the nurses (Gayla was one – nice name) came to change my colostomy pouch system. That was an experience. And thank the Lord for my daughter, Gayla. She had brought my purse that had a complete replacement colostomy pouch set in it. I had to guide the nurses on how to do the change. I kept falling asleep on them, or passing out, whatever. My daughters would wake me up. They finally got it changed and got me all cleaned up. I felt so good.

I did have one regret though. When my daughter asked me if I wanted her to read my Bible to me, I replied no. I cannot imagine why I said no. Maybe it was because I could not stay awake long enough to hear the words. I do love to read my Bible.

Please forgive me for this, dear Lord. I asked Gina's forgiveness also. Please don't let go of my hand, Lord.

As more fluids flowed through my body, I was able to stay awake for longer periods of time. The doctors decided I needed to be admitted to the hospital, though. I needed to have lab tests and vitals monitored every thirty minutes. The hospital had no medical rooms available, so they put me in the SICU where I received great care. I do not remember much else about Sunday, but on Monday, Dr. Hartwell came to see me. She was so upset with me. She really chewed me out. She said I had great kids and smart kids who knew what to do. She said I needed to relinquish control to them when they knew what was best for me. She said Raymond was my hero. If he had not come to check on me Sunday morning, I probably would have been gone in a few hours! What an eye-opener. I did not realize I was in such bad shape and so close to death. Raymond did and Gayla did too. I just would not let him call the doctor. Now, he knows, as do the other kids, that he and they can do what they know is right. Even if I disagree, they can make the decisions that need to be made. Boy, that was a hard pill to swallow. Now my kids look out for me, instead of my looking out for them. Changing life roles is difficult for all of us, but necessary at times. I love my children and their families very much.

Thank You, Lord, for my family and my doctors.

As the fluids flowed through my veins and the blood tests continued, my liver count started going down to normal. I knew it would. Chip and Fran made a safe trip from their vacation to the hospital SICU where I was. I began staying awake longer, but I still could not get out of bed. In fact, I do not think I got out of that hospital bed until Tuesday when they were ready to let me go home. That was an experience also. The SICU usually does not release patients to go home. They release them to another part of the hospital. It took awhile to round up the necessary paperwork to release me, but they were so good there.

Thank You, Lord, for those great nurses. Please bless them as they continue nursing.

We checked on the new medicine that I had started taking the previous Friday. We found that it had several side effects, including confusion, disorientation and dehydration. We added those side effects to my other problems of not drinking enough water, vomiting, diarrhea and extreme fatigue. We realized this was the perfect formula for the dehydration and negative reaction to chemotherapy treatments that put me in the hospital. We therefore discarded that medicine.

My children decided that I should not be alone when I got home on Tuesday, January 31, 2006. They arranged for one of them or a friend to stay with me during the day and night for several days. It was so different, having someone there when I was doing nothing but sleeping. I was actually embarrassed about it.

Thank You, Lord, for family and friends, Linda, Tammy, Velda and others. Bless each of them.

Of course, I had to miss that week's chemotherapy treatment. But I soon got back on the regular routine. I completed the seven months of chemotherapy treatments. This resulted in **complete remission of the cancer again.** This was the third time I had to take chemotherapy treatments for colorectal cancer. It was my fifth attack of cancer. This remission lasted for one year and one month.

Hold my hand, Lord.

Another happy event occurred in May 2006. Our granddaughter, Tarah, and Christopher were married.

Thank You, Lord, for the gift of marriage and for increasing our family. Bless their lives together with You.

CHAPTER 13

MY THIRD RECURRENCE OF CANCER

That brings us to May of 2007. After a regularly scheduled PET scan, I was told that same spot/area was growing again. In June more tests – a bone scan, colonoscopy via colostomy, and rectal exam – resulted in an "all clear." Those tests said there was no cancer activity. But the PET scan had said yes, there was activity. The Standardized Uptake Valve (SUV) was 13.8, which I understood was high. This was so confusing. So, where was this cancer activity? What were we going to do about it? How could we get rid of it?

Dr. Mattar wanted to see if I might be a candidate for the new CyberKnife radiation treatment. This new machine had only been in the local area for not quite a year. However, the conference with the CyberKnife radiation specialist was discouraging. I probably could not have this treatment. A stationary target was needed. The "hot spot" in me was moving. Or, at least, the exact location could not be pinpointed at that time. My remaining organs had rearranged themselves inside my abdominal cavity. This was due to all the previous radiations and surgeries I had. The CyberKnife specialist would not and could not shoot at a moving target. I agreed. I did not want him to do that. Plus, I had already had three other types of radiation. We would wait two months and have another CT scan to see if the spot/area had grown large enough to be seen on the scan. If it had not, we would continue to wait. If the spot/area was big enough and did show up, the exact location could be pinpointed. Then we could design the plan of attack.

Maybe You, good Lord, will decide to remove that spot/area entirely before the next exam. That would be the greatest. Nevertheless, not my will, but Thy will, be done, oh Lord.

In July of 2007, one more happy event occurred. Our grandson, James got married.

Thank You, Lord, for this gift of marriage also. Bless their lives together and keep them in Your care.

Life continues on. Life does not stop and wait for anything like tests for cancer. Life is always in the present. I cannot re-live life that is past. I cannot live life that is in the future. **I can only live life in the now.** That is what my Lord wants me to do. He wants me to get to know Him intimately by reading His Word. This is so that I know what He expects of me. He wants me to know how I should use the gifts His Holy Spirit has given me in my life to serve Him. He wants me to talk to Him through my prayers. He calls me His daughter. What child does not want to imitate their father? He is the King of Kings. That makes me His princess.

Please help me to be more like You, my living Lord. Help me to be a conduit of Your light and love to others.

You have blessed me so much, Lord. You have given me a wonderful and loving and believing family and so many friends. You have given me a great life here on earth, with all its challenges and Your already-planned results and rewards. You have given me a future eternal life with You – and with my loved ones who are already with You in Heaven. I humbly ask that You hold my precious family in Your forgiving and loving arms as You lead them through their wild rides called life. Keep them close to You, Lord. Guide, discipline, protect, love, and bless them. Help all of us to use our lives for You. We need to help others know You and Your Gift of Eternal Life through faith in Your Son, Jesus Christ. Help us to help others to know that we are all only temporary residents of earth. Our home is in Heaven with You. I humbly ask that You use me as You see fit, to share You with others here on earth. Thank You, Lord, for this great gift of earthly life. I love my life. What more can I thank You for?

I have been truly blessed throughout my life. I am so grateful that God has given me these many years. I truly thank Him for my children and their families whom I love so very much: Gayla and John; Gary; Gina and Goran; Glynne' and Bill; Raymond and Jennifer; Joshua and boys (Gage, Braden, Garrett, Grant, Josh, Jr.); Tarah and Christopher; James; Jared; Tanner; Trae;

Rachael; Mariah; Oliver; Libby; Cole; Sam; and Jack. I thank Him also for my brother, Chip, and Fran and their children, Sherri, Shelli, and Andrew; for Earle's sister Nan and her family; Earle's brother Charles and his family; and Earle's sister Barbara's three girls and their families. I am so thankful for the wonderful aunts and cousins, other relatives, and the many, many friends whom I also love.

Just saying thank You, Lord, does not seem good enough. Praising You for all You have done for me does not seem good enough either. It is my joy to glorify You as much as I can in my life, but You know, Lord, that I always come asking for Your help. You are the almighty Creator, Savior, and Sustainer/Comforter of this entire world and everything and everybody in it. You are the only true God. You are the only way to eternal life with You in Heaven. Thank You for Your unconditional love for me. Thank You for being merciful to me, a poor miserable sinner. Thank You for Your grace. Please do not forget that I love You and my family very much. Please help me to live my life for You.

Hold my hand, Lord. Please hold the hands of all the doctors, nurses, and technicians who will be on my team to fight this cancer again. You, Lord, are the General of this war. You can win it with just Your spoken Word. You are almighty, powerful, forgiving, and loving. You know everything. I pray for Your guidance for me and for all of us and for Your perfect will to be done. I am trusting You, Lord, to lead me through this next journey also. And, as we go through this battle together, please always

Hold My Hand, Lord!

CHAPTER 14

THE CYBERKNIFE

And my journey goes on…..so very much has happened between August 2007 and August 2009.

To review, the PET scan in May 2007 showed a "hot spot" growing again. The colonoscopy in June 2007 showed no evidence of malignancy inside the colon. This meant that the area/spot/mass/tumor was not inside the colon. But where was it? Dr. Mattar scheduled a CT scan in early August 2007. I received the results in his office. The mass did show up that time in the CT scan also. The blood work confirmed it was not inside the colon. That meant the mass was outside the colon and still in the pelvic floor – the original site.

Praise to You, merciful Lord, that it is not in a new site.

The spot/mass/area/tumor had not metastasized. We knew this spot/mass could always recur, which it kept doing. This was the **third recurrence of colorectal cancer – my sixth attack of all cancers.** We remembered that during the original colon surgery on October 31, 2000, the surgeon, Dr. Hunt, advised us she could not scrape out all of the tumor. It was too close to nerves and could have debilitated me. All my doctors had told me that this tumor, and subsequently colorectal cancer, was caused by the build up of scar tissue from the first radiation treatments in 1975. Data had shown that most radiation problems occurred five to fifteen years after the radiation. I was given twenty-five years before problems occurred.

Thank You so very much, Lord. Keep holding my hand, Lord.

Dr. Mattar and I had a serious talk. I felt that my body could not withstand a fourth round of months of chemotherapy treatments. My thinking was that at some point my body was going to say, "Whoa Gwen. It's not going to work. I can't take any more chemotherapy. That's enough." And then, what would I do? The chemotherapy treatments were just not killing that spot. They would only put it in remission for awhile. Eventually that spot would start growing again. Dr. Mattar agreed with me. He now felt that I really might be a candidate for the new CyberKnife radiation treatment and wanted me to revisit the specialist doctors. So, I did.

Again, I thank You, Lord, for Dr. Mattar and the medical skills You have blessed him with.

Another PET scan was scheduled. Then a CT/abdomen/PET fusion scan was scheduled. Then another appointment with a CyberKnife Specialist was scheduled. Then another appointment with Dr. Mattar was scheduled. These appointments took me into September. Dr. Mattar was finally assured I could have the CyberKnife radiation treatment. This should kill that remaining mass/growth/area/spot. This new technology was amazing. If needed, I would have another round of chemotherapy treatments. But it would include lesser doses of only two chemicals. Again, it is God's Will, not mine. I feel great. I am so blessed. I will keep hanging onto the Lord's Hand through all of this.

I praise and thank You, Lord, for this new treatment. I also thank You for all the prayers of my family and friends. I am so grateful for them and for You holding my hand.

On August 30, 2007, I saw the CyberKnife Oncologist, a great doctor, intelligent, caring, and well-respected in the CyberKnife community. She said they could help me, if I wanted them to, but there were risks. The CyberKnife is a robotic arm that shoots a beam of radiation precisely to a specific target. The beam is released multiple times from several different angles. This beam hits a pin-point spot, as opposed to other types of radiation that hit a wide area. The other types of radiation were what I had before in 1975. These caused the problem that I was dealing with now. However, the CyberKnife beam was so direct, it was supposed to do very little damage to surrounding tissue. Of course, there are always risks. Those risks for me included a perforated bowel and bleeding if they should nick the adjoining bowel. In that case, they would need to do major surgery to fix it. That is okay with me because if I did not have the CyberKnife treatments, eventually the tumor was going to grow into the bowel anyway. Then it would cause big problems of the same kind that could happen from the CyberKnife.

Now I had a choice to make. Should I take the chemotherapy treatments again, knowing the side effects? It was my thinking that they could not completely eliminate the tumor. Past experiences had shown me that it would probably continue to grow into the surrounding tissue and nerves anyway. My other choice was to step out in faith, knowing the possible consequences, to trust in our Lord, and have this new CyberKnife radiation treatment now. To me, the risks were about the same. I really thought since I had so many chemotherapy treatments already, one of these days my body was going to reject the chemicals. Then I would be in big trouble. Plus, each round of months of chemotherapy treatments had been harder on my body than the previous. I remembered my hospitalization in January 2006. This would be my **fourth round of treatments for colorectal cancer.**

I compared this to the CyberKnife treatments which have almost no side effects. There is no pain, no incision, no blood loss, no anesthesia, no nausea, no diarrhea, and no recovery time. I could immediately return to normal activity. My level of energy may go down for awhile. However, my energy level would not be nearly as down from the radiation, as it would be from the chemotherapy treatments again. And, of course there was always the possibility of risks that could damage my body during the treatments. I considered all these issues and prayed to my Lord for guidance. I decided to step out in faith and have the CyberKnife treatments. I was excited. I asked God to use this method to rid my body entirely of this awful cancer. I prayed that this was His will.

Nevertheless, not my will, but Your will be done, Lord. Thank You, Lord, for always holding my hand.

So, the treatment planning part started on September 12, 2007. First, I was fitted in a body mold. It was something like a soft bean bag bed that I laid on while fully clothed. They vacuumed/ suctioned out the air. The bean bag bed then became very hard. It had actually molded into the shape of my body. I was to lie in that mold for all the tests and the subsequent treatments. I was not to move. My body had to be in the same position each time for the tests and for the CyberKnife machine to direct beams of radiation to the target. This was sci-fi stuff. They did another CT scan and MRI to get the correct measurements and information needed. This data was then input into the computer of the CyberKnife machine. The beam could then be directed to the exact target. The machine had a huge, movable, rotating arm that directed the beam to the tumor from several different angles. That is why I had to lay perfectly still and not move. I was to have three treatments – they were called "fractions" – about one to two hours each. There would be one fraction a day for three days. The schedule of which days depended upon the availability of the CyberKnife machine. After the treatments were finished, there would be follow-up tests, about a month apart, to verify the absence of cancer. I had to keep remembering this was the tentative plan. It could always be revised. I had hoped that by year's end, this would all be over, and I would be free of cancer.

Lord, you know how excited I am. You know the risks and You already know the outcome. No matter what, please continue holding my hand.

The plan was finalized, at least for now. I would have three CyberKnife radiation treatments, about two hours each, on September 19, 21 and 25 (Wednesday, Friday and Tuesday). We would wait for a month while the radiation continued to do its work. Did you know that radiation continues radiating for a few months after you have finished the treatments? There would be follow-up tests. If necessary, I might need to start six months of chemotherapy treatments again, beginning about mid October. My sons and daughters would be helping me out again. I would not be going alone.

Thank You, Lord, for my precious sons and daughters. And, thank You, Lord, for the prayers of family and friends. Please give each of them a special blessing.

It is my understanding that the CyberKnife machine converts high energy electricity into radiation – ionization. It is like a chest X-ray, only six hundred times as powerful. The CyberKnife is exact and directs beams precisely to a target with very little "scatter" to the surrounding areas. The CyberKnife is ionizing radiation. The GammaKnife is cobalt radiation. In 1975, I had three types of radiation: cobalt, radium and X-ray.

The X-ray treatments back in 1975 were not nearly as powerful as the CyberKnife. Neither were any of these other radiations as precise as the CyberKnife radiation. I do have pictures of the CyberKnife radiation machine and the room where it was located. I share these interesting and informative pictures when I speak at groups. The CyberKnife is an impressive machine.

I did complete the three CyberKnife radiation treatments as scheduled. Again, one or two of my children took me to each treatment. Everything went as planned. I had no trouble or side effects, except for losing a little energy. Or so I thought. We had changed the timing plan for testing and follow-up chemotherapy treatments. We wanted to allow the radiation to do its work first. So, here we go again – the waiting game.

In October 2007, the CT scan showed the tumor was shrinking, and the CEA count was less than 0.5, which was great news. This meant that the CyberKnife radiation was doing its job.

I thank and praise You, Lord, for this successful treatment. Keep holding my hand, Lord.

The radiation would continue for several more months. Dr. Mattar wanted to wait a few weeks and then have another PET scan. This scan would show if there was any hot spot or cancer activity remaining. If there was activity, he would start me on chemotherapy treatments again. If there was no activity, I would not have to take any more chemotherapy. I was excited. It was difficult to wait for the results.

I thank all my family and friends for praying for me. Praying is the most important thing you can do for someone. Our family had a wonderful and blessed Thanksgiving and Christmas season.

Thank You, Lord, for holding all our hands. And, thank You, Lord, for the technology You have blessed us with, such as this CyberKnife radiation machine. I praise You for holding my hand through all these challenges. I thank You that You have always provided support for me. I feel so blessed.

On November 28, 2007, Dr. Mattar said the PET scan was good and showed no activity. **This third recurrence of colorectal cancer was in remission again. This was my sixth bout with cancer and cancer treatments.**

Thank You, dear Lord.

This was what we prayed for and had wanted. No more chemotherapy, no more radiation. Life was indeed good. I was to wait three months for the next tests. I felt that the cancer was dead, that the CyberKnife radiation treatments had killed it.

Oh, dear Lord, please continue holding my hand. I do not know what is in the future.

I also thought of these bouts of cancer as episodes or attacks of cancer. I knew that the Holy Bible, God's Word, considers seven to be the number of completion. So, I wondered....

CHAPTER 15

SIDE AND AFTER EFFECTS OF TREATMENTS

During the next couple of months, I experienced several bouts of severe cramps, nausea, diarrhea, and vomiting. My doctor and I could not figure out why this was happening to me. We were trying different foods, different amounts of food, different times to eat, different antacids, and more. Nothing seemed to help. We knew my intestines were trying to heal from the surgery. If this problem kept up, I would have to have more tests.

I was living life, doing all the things I wanted. I was enjoying my family, children, grandchildren, great-grandchildren, aunts, cousins, and my friends. I was very active in my church and a cancer support organization. I had also joined an organization in the county to help abused children while they were going through the legal system. Life was very busy. It never dawned on me that my intestinal problems could be from some of the risks of surgery that I had been warned about. I guess I thought that any problems would have shown up immediately, not months later. The time came when I could not eat and keep any food down. Normally I am a big – and good – eater. Nothing slows down my appetite. Even during the months of chemotherapy treatments, I still had a fairly good appetite. Now, though, my intestinal problems kept getting worse until I just could not eat at all.

I called my surgeon, Dr. Hunt, on the morning of Friday, February 22, 2008. I explained the situation and all that we had tried to do to help me. She asked me where I was. She knew how active I always was. I told her I was still in bed, that I really did not feel well. She told me to have one of my daughters take me directly to the hospital now. She would meet us there. I was to have a CT scan of my abdomen so she would know what was happening to me. She wanted to rule out radiation necrosis. My daughter, Glynne', took me. At the hospital I was given barium to drink for the CT scan. I did not think I could get it down, but I did. The scan showed a huge blockage in my abdomen. It also showed that my stomach was as big as a football. Dr. Hunt said she was admitting me to the hospital right then. She told the nurses to get me to a room immediately. They were to put down a Nasogastric (NG) tube, because I was going to blow. They did and I did. Oh how awful. What a mess. She also said that surgery was required. It would not be done until Monday.

This would be my **second colon resection surgery**. There would need to be more tests first. They needed to keep my colon and stomach emptied before the surgery. Needless to say, I did not get anything to eat or drink. I did get fluids from the IV though. I do not remember very much about the weekend. So many precious friends and family came to visit me or called me.

Thank You, Lord, for all my family and friends and these wonderful doctors and nurses.

The X-rays showed that the barium was moving very, very slowly through my system. It was being blocked before reaching the colon. However, it was not a complete blockage. There was some barium seeping through. The nurses and my daughters kept very good care of me.

Thank You, Lord. You are such a gracious and merciful God.

On Sunday, February 24, 2008, Dr. Hunt advised us that she could not do the surgery via laparoscope. She would have to make an incision, which she would try to keep below my belly button. I did not care about another scar. She would most likely have to remove twelve inches of my small intestine by cutting it out and then reattaching the intestines. She might have to remove the ileocecal valve also. This is between the small intestine and large intestine – also called the colon. She suspected damage from radiation necrosis. My intestines were as hard as concrete. The risks – because there are always risks – included a high risk of infection, a leak, and a slight risk of requiring a temporary ileostomy. This involved the connection between the small and large intestines. It is similar to a colostomy, but in a different location. This would be a second pouch for me. Good grief. That would mean I would be a two-pouch lady. I did not even want to think about that.

Hold my hand tightly, Lord.

On Monday, February 25, 2008, Dr. Hunt performed the successful surgery. She removed twenty-three inches of my small intestine, the ileocecal value, the appendix, and another four to six inches of the colon. She said there literally was a clump of intestines that had hardened together – that was the football. Because of the previous surgeries I had, the intestines and colon had dropped down and got in the way of the CyberKnife radiation. So part of them got "zapped" also. This was one of the risks I was told could happen. Little did we know that other organs had also dropped down and were "zapped." This had done quite a bit of damage that I had to deal with later.

Dr. Hunt did not need to do an ileostomy. I was so thankful for that. She had also cut and used the same scar in my abdomen – from my belly button to my pelvis – that had been used for the hysterectomy in 1992 and the colon resection and colostomy in 2000. One of my daughters suggested that I maybe needed a zipper there – ha. But now I did not have my soul-mate Honey Earle to remove the staples. Dr. Hunt told me that food would not stay very long in my shortened intestines. I needed to eat healthy. I would lose weight. And I did start losing weight.

This surgery marked the seventh time I had dealt with cancer and the side or after effects of treatments. I remembered that **in God's Word, seven is the number of completion. I thought, "Am I now completely through with cancer?"** I really felt the cancer was gone, not just in remission. But what do I know? God is so good. Our Heavenly Father, Son Jesus Christ, and Holy Spirit have been with me through all these years of dealing with cancers. Does this surgery count as the seventh attack of cancer, I wondered.

Almighty, Triune God, I thank You for loving me and holding my hand always. You have held my hand not just through these cancer years, but my entire life.

In February of 2008, while I was still in the hospital, my grandson James had a daughter he named Payton. I finally had my first great-granddaughter, to add to my five great-grandsons.

Thank You, Lord, for another beautiful gift of life. Please help James to be the kind of father You want him to be.

On Monday, March 2, 2008, I was released from the hospital. Gayla took me to Raymond and Jennifer's home. I stayed for two weeks to recuperate from this last surgery. They took such good care of me. Jennifer even learned how to clean my incision and pack it twice a day. I had developed an infection at one end of it. She did an excellent job and it healed quickly.

I so enjoyed my time with them and with my grandchildren. I finally had to tell them I needed to go home. I loved being in their home so much. I was getting too used to being there. I certainly did not want to wear out my welcome. They assured me I would not.

Thank You again, Lord, for all my children, their families, and their help. Thank You, Lord, for a sweet, caring, and loving daughter-in-law and family.

Chapter 16

Life Goes On

I began feeling so much better. Life again returned to normal, whatever normal is. Yes, I did have consequences from the CyberKnife radiation treatments and had to have major abdominal surgery, but I knew I would have the CyberKnife radiation treatments again, if necessary. Yes, I would. I told the doctors and nurses and technicians at the CyberKnife Center that I was their best cheerleader. In my opinion, what happened to me was not an intended result of the CyberKnife radiation treatments. It was a risk I took, knowing there was a danger of zapping other organs if they got too close to the spot to be radiated. The rearrangement of my organs was caused by my previous treatments and surgeries. They got in the way, so they got zapped, but I still feel and believe and know I made the best decision. I did begin losing weight – which is not a bad thing as far as I was concerned at that time.

Early in April 2008, I was interviewed by Jarrett Medlin, the editor of "WICHITA!" magazine. He was doing a series of seven medical breakthroughs. He wanted to feature the new radiation treatment by the CyberKnife machine as one of them. He had heard so much about it. The hospital had recommended he interview me. The July 2008 issue was published and released with my article in it, along with the other six medical breakthroughs. I was so very pleased with the article he wrote. He had actually included my faith in our Triune God. He also had noted that I was so thankful to our Lord for His healing of my cancers. I was so excited about being in a magazine that I bought issues for all my family. What fun that was.

Thank You, Lord, for Jarrett's faithful reporting. Thank You also for this great and wonderful opportunity to witness for You.

All my tests, PET scans, CT scans, mammogram, and laboratory work, from May through November 2008 were negative. **There was no sign of cancer. It was still in remission.** It was really gone, as far as I was concerned.

Thank You, Lord.

But I began having occasional bladder infections or urinary tract infections (UTIs). As the months rolled by, these UTIs became more frequent. Dr. Hartwell was treating them with various antibiotics that would heal the infection each time.

Life took over again. Life moves on, you know. We lost precious loved ones – too many of both family and friends. Then, I needed to have some dental work that my insurance would not cover. I got a temporary, part-time job at a radio station – country music, of course – just two blocks from my home. I started there in August of 2008, and enjoyed it very much. I was still losing weight, which was okay with me. I was still doing everything I thought I wanted to do, including exercising and keeping so busy. I completed the dental work, but then I had to get a newer vehicle. My Ford F150 pickup, "Big Red," was too old and had too many miles and needed too much repair. I decided to continue working part-time in order to buy a new vehicle.

Something was still nagging at me, though. I did not feel quite right. I cannot explain what I felt. I just knew that all was not well yet. I could not figure out what was bothering me. Was it my family, my friends, my still missing my soul-mate Earle? Was it me? I thought I had dealt with cancer seven times now, considering six attacks of cancer and one extra surgery. I thought I was through with cancer. It's gone, right? But what was bothering me? So, I kept busy, so busy that I was not paying attention to myself – again.

Help me through this also, dear Lord.

About two weeks after I had a flu shot on October 29, 2008, I became ill again and missed work. I was so tired and out of sorts. I thought it was a reaction to the flu shot. But it was another UTI. I got antibiotics for it again. This time even two different medicines did not work. We were having our family Thanksgiving on November 27 at my son Gary's home. Each of us brings our favorite food/dish. My family are all wonderful cooks. I managed to get there with the turkey, but I could not do anything else. I was so exhausted. All my children and their families were there, except for one grandson and his family. I could not even play with my precious grandchildren and great-grandchildren – my favorite thing to do, along with visiting with my sons and daughters. I was so extremely tired that I just rested on the couch. My daughter Gina realized that I also had a fever. She talked with the others. They all decided I needed to go to the hospital ER.

As I remember it, Gina and Glynne' took me. The ER found that I was dehydrated and started an IV. They also did some blood work that confirmed the UTI. Then, they took a CT scan and told us that I had a **very, very bad infection that was in my urethra, bladder, both ureters, and both kidneys.** Of course, they contacted my doctor, Dr. Hartwell. They gave me a powerful antibiotic and inserted a catheter to empty my bladder. Then the ER sent me home with the catheter inserted and two different sized containers, one each for day and night. I was so glad I did not have to stay in the hospital.

Thank You, Lord. Keep holding my hand, please.

I did not get to go home, though, I was taken to the home of Glynne', then to the home of Gayla. I stayed over the weekend and did nothing but sleep. They took good care of me, as always. I had the catheter in for twelve days. That was interesting. The hospital also did a follow-up renal sonogram on December 22. This showed the infection going away. It was then that I realized I had very little energy. I simply could not do what I had done before. I could not keep up with all my activities any more. Something had changed inside of me, and, I was losing so much more weight.

At this point, I had fatigue beyond anything I ever had before – even during the chemotherapy treatments. I also had shortness of breath. This concerned my doctors and they wanted me to see several specialists, including lung, heart and kidney. So began another regime of visiting doctors and more tests/procedures.

A pulmonologist said my lungs were clear. My shortness of breath was not connected to my lungs. He thought my problems were connected to the severe kidney infection, dehydration, and extreme fatigue I had experienced in November and December. He recommended that I go back and exercise at this special women's exercise place. It took me quite a while to get the energy to do that again.

A cardiologist did an EKG and an echo-cardiogram. Both these tests were normal. My heart was fine. He also said my shortness of breath was due to the severe kidney infection. He was so excited that he and his wife were blessed with a baby girl in March.

Praise be to You, Heavenly Father, for another precious life. And, Thank You, Lord, for these good test results.

A urogynecology and restorative pelvic surgeon determined the damage was above the area that he would treat. He recommended I see a urologist. From the procedures he did, however, he had noted that my bladder was not draining properly. This was causing the pesky and recurrent UTIs. We now know the bladder damage was caused by all the radiations I had.

The urologist did a sonogram with a camera in my bladder. This showed the radiation damage to the urethra and bladder. I got to watch the procedure on a screen. It was so interesting and informative. I asked him what the pink spots were on my white bladder. He said that the **bladder should be all pink.** The white spots were radiation damage. He said that my bladder harness and muscles were good. But the urethra had also been damaged. It was constricted by the radiation, therefore, the bladder could not empty properly. This was causing urine to remain in the bladder. That stale urine backed up into the ureters and on up into the kidneys. This then caused the UTIs. Other tests verified I still had the UTI. He prescribed another antibiotic and some other medications. These should hopefully relieve some of my problems. He wanted me to return in six months, in July 2009, for another renal sonogram. I did. I had another UTI, and my bladder still would not empty completely. So, now I was put on a daily maintenance antibiotic, plus some other medications to try and help the bladder empty. This would hopefully keep infections away. All the medications I was on had to do with cancer side effects and after effects of treatments. Otherwise, I was healthy, and I had gained back some weight.

Thank You, Lord, for all my doctors. Praise be to You, Lord.

In between all these specialists, I was seeing my family doctor, Dr. Hartwell, on a regular basis. She and her husband Rick had been blessed with two sons, two grandsons, and three granddaughters. I was also regularly seeing my oncologist, Dr. Mattar. He and his wife Rita were blessed with two sons and two daughters.

Thank You, Lord, for these two special doctors whom I love and their wonderful families.

Other good events had occurred in my family. My granddaughter, Tarah, and husband Christopher had a sweet baby girl, Trinity, in March of 2009, my second great-granddaughter.

Thank You, Lord, for yet another precious child to raise in Your shadow. Please be with Christopher and Tarah to guide them always.

Another wonderful event occurred in June of 2009. My grandson, Jared, married Tori.

Thank You again, Lord, for another happy marriage. Please bless and be with them also.

In mid-summer of 2009, that "something had happened inside of me" feeling surfaced again. I questioned myself, "Am I finally through with cancer?" It was then I realized that I was taking better care of myself. I was being more aware of what I was doing. I was learning how to say "No" when I needed to. I was talking, through prayer, to my LORD, and listening to Him, through reading His Word. I felt healthy again, for the first time in many years. I was gaining weight also. I did not look so frail and sickly.

I like quietness in my home when I am by myself. I can hear that "still, small voice" encourage me and urge me on to what I should do for Him. But, I also love for my family and friends to be here in my home. I love all the noise, busy-ness, laughter, and love that goes on.

Thank You especially, Lord, for this wonderful family you blessed me with. Thank You for their love for me, for each other, and for You. Please bless them with Your forgiveness, guidance, presence, and love.

Awareness dawned on me during this time that I was actually making plans for the future. I was enjoying life again. What a realization. As He had told me once, ***"Relax, Gwen, I am in control,"*** I am relaxing. Is the cancer finally gone? I do not know. But I choose to believe it is. Yes, I have some side effects or after effects from all the treatments. But I can deal with them, with the help of my Lord, doctors, family, and friends. I have come to grips with the fact that I am by myself, without my soul-mate Honey Earle. But I know I am never alone. Now, I must and I am getting on with my life. There's so much I can do for my Lord, who kept me alive on earth to work for Him.

Dear Lord, I pray that my family and friends will benefit from my journey through these cancers. I pray that they will trust You with their lives also.

My prayer is also that You, Lord, will always guide/lead me where You want me to go. I know that where You guide, You provide. Thank You so very much, Lord Jesus, for my earthly life. And, until You take me home with You to Heaven, please always hold my hand, Lord, and help me to

Love Others As You Love Them!

ABOUT THE AUTHOR

Gwen Hensley is a God-fearing woman who has been attacked by three different types of cancer and three recurrences of one cancer. Because of Gwen's faith in her Lord, positive attitude, and determination to survive, her doctors suggested she write her story to encourage others also going through traumatic  diagnoses. **_Hold My Hand, Lord!_** is her first published writing. Gwen does not claim to be an author. She is simply speaking to you through her words, as if she were visiting at your kitchen table and drinking a cup of coffee or tea with you.

Gwen is a native of Kansas. As she says, "I was born, bred, wed, and widowed right here in Kansas." She now lives by herself in the country near Rose Hill. She and her late husband had planned on retiring there. Her five children keep very good watch of her. They and her grandchildren and great-grandchildren are her joy. She remains involved in Bible studies in her church and still does volunteer work.

Gwen shares her faith, as well as her journey through cancers, with everyone she can. She encourages others to put their trust in the only One who can truly help, our Lord God Almighty.

As King David spoke in song to the Lord on the day the Lord delivered him from the hand of all his enemies, Gwen, too, sings praises to her Savior for delivering her from her enemy, cancer. As she continues on her life's journey, she prays that you will be encouraged by her words, and that in your life's journey, you will also ask:

"Hold My Hand, Lord!"

Printed and bound by PG in the USA